THE LEGO® BUILD-IT BOOK
AMAZING VEHICLES

The LEGO® Build-It Book, Vol. 1: Amazing Vehicles.
Copyright © 2013 by Nathanaël Kuipers and Mattia Zamboni.

Printed in China

First printing

17 16 15 14 13   1 2 3 4 5 6 7 8 9

ISBN-10: 1-59327-503-X
ISBN-13: 978-1-59327-503-7

Publisher: William Pollock
Production Editor: Riley Hoffman
Model Design: Nathanaël Kuipers
Cover and Interior Design: Mattia Zamboni
Cartoon Illustration: Pasquale D'Silva
Developmental Editor: Tyler Ortman
Proofreader: Paula L. Fleming

For information on distribution, translations, or bulk sales, please contact No Starch Press, Inc. directly:

No Starch Press, Inc.
38 Ringold Street, San Francisco, CA 94103
phone: 415.863.9900; fax: 415.863.9950; info@nostarch.com; www.nostarch.com

Library of Congress Cataloging-in-Publication Data
A catalog record of this book is available from the Library of Congress.

Production Date: 03/29/2013
Plant & Location: Printed by Everbest Printing (Guangzhou, China), Co. Ltd
Job / Batch #: 110939.2

THE LEGO® BUILD-IT BOOK
AMAZING VEHICLES

Nathanaël Kuipers — Mattia Zamboni

no starch press

About the authors

Nathanaël Kuipers
Model Designer

Nathanaël Kuipers is a Dutch design professional who worked for several years as a product developer for the LEGO Group in Denmark, where he was mainly responsible for engineering LEGO Technic models. He is the mastermind behind models like #8261, #8271, #8272, #8292, and #8674. He has also collaborated on the creation of many other models. Check out his work at *http://www.nkubate.com/*.

Mattia Zamboni
Graphic Artist

Mattia Zamboni is a fan of graphic design, photography, and LEGO, and he has a degree in electrical engineering. Based in Switzerland, he pursues his passion of graphic design, showcasing his talents within the world of 3D computer graphic arts. Check out his work at *http://www.brickpassion.com/*.

Acknowledgments

From Nathanaël:

First I'd like to thank Mattia Zamboni for his enthusiasm, dedication, and friendship. If it weren't for him, this book would never have looked this good and perhaps would never have seen the light of day. I'd also like to thank the LEGO Group for their great toy and for giving me the opportunity of a lifetime: to design several official models, which made me a better builder.

Furthermore I thank my parents for their unconditional love and support and for giving me several LEGO sets to build with as a child so I was able to express and develop my creative side; Joe Meno for his support in publishing some of my models and for introducing me to No Starch Press; and No Starch Press for believing in an idea and for providing this great opportunity to share my knowledge.

And of course, a big "Thank you!" to all the fans who have given their support from around the world, motivating me to write a book. Your kind and encouraging words have kept me going during difficult times!

From Mattia:

My biggest thanks go to Nelson Painço for his advice on improving my 3D graphics and the images you see in this book. Thanks also to my son, Leonardo, who has been an excellent play tester despite his young age, and to my sweet wife, Fabiola, who has supported this project from the beginning. Special thanks go to Pasquale D'Silva for very kindly providing the quirky character for this book. And last but not least, I am grateful to Nathanaël for being such a great inspiration with his models!

About the book

"Just imagine!"

Sometimes it's not as easy as it sounds, is it? Well, help is on the way. In this book, you'll find the secrets of a true master builder—so be prepared for some pretty advanced techniques.

Because we don't want to bore you with theory, our focus is on building in practice, guiding you with step-by-step instructions. By creatively using the same pieces in 10 different configurations, you'll see the amazing potential of the LEGO brick.

We hope that this book helps you to discover the many possibilities that the LEGO system has to offer, unleashing your creativity and inspiring you to create your own original models!

What you need

Every project in this book uses a common set of pieces—a complete list is shown in the Bill of Materials on the facing page. If you have set #5867, the LEGO CREATOR Super Speedster, you have all the bricks you need.

If you have a collection of other LEGO sets and want to determine which pieces you're missing from set #5867, we recommend using Rebrickable (*http://rebrickable .com/*). To buy the parts you're missing, you have a few options.

If you're not lucky enough to live near an official LEGO retail store with a "Pick a Brick" wall, you can buy individual pieces online (*http://shop.lego.com/en-US/ Pick-A-Brick-ByTheme*). You can also buy LEGO pieces from BrickLink (*http://www .bricklink.com/*), a comprehensive, international marketplace for buying new and used bricks.

Don't forget that you can use parts in different colors or with similar shapes, too. That's what's so cool about building with LEGO bricks! You can always redesign and customize everything using your own imagination.

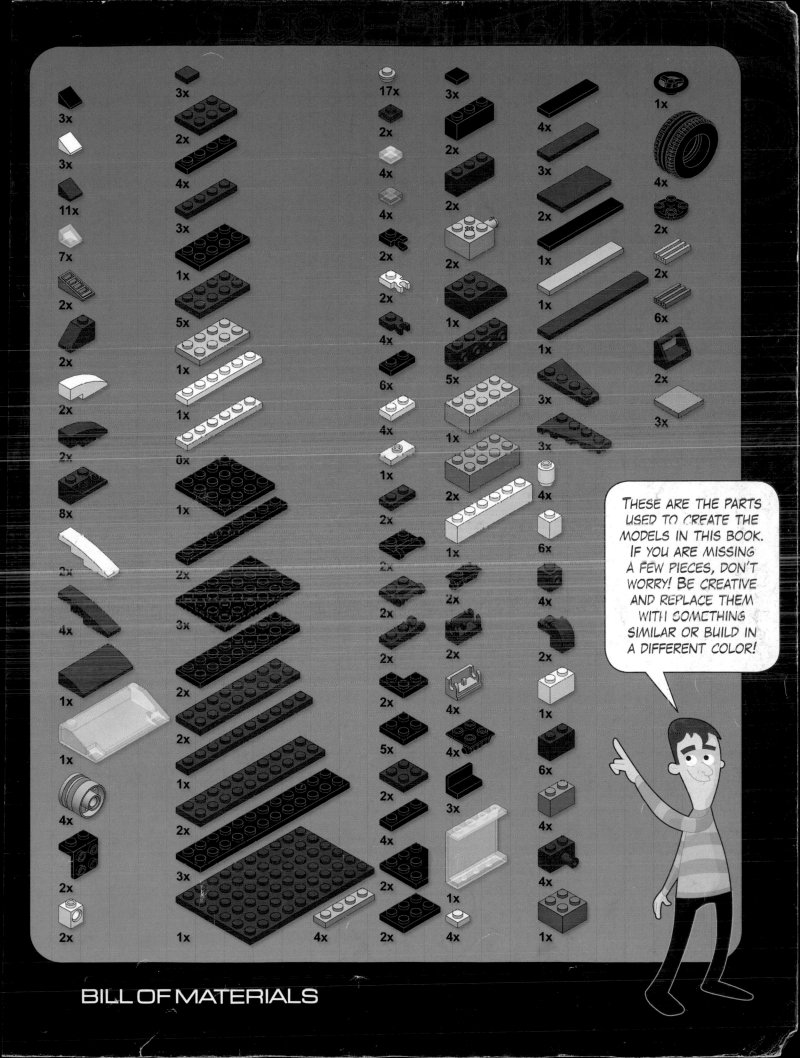

THESE ARE THE PARTS USED TO CREATE THE MODELS IN THIS BOOK. IF YOU ARE MISSING A FEW PIECES, DON'T WORRY! BE CREATIVE AND REPLACE THEM WITH SOMETHING SIMILAR OR BUILD IN A DIFFERENT COLOR!

BILL OF MATERIALS

||CONTENTS

BUILDING BASICS

Getting Creative with Parts

When you're building, it really doesn't matter what bricks you start with. The most important thing is to be creative with the materials you have.

With a little imagination, even the simplest elements can have an amazing variety of uses.

Engine Pistons

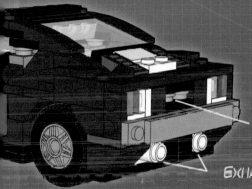

License Plate

Exhaust Pipes

Logo for the Grille

Springs

Shock Absorbers

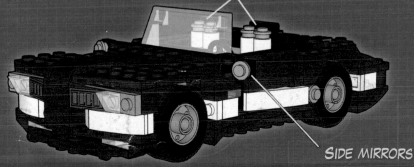

Chairs

Side mirrors

THE LEGO BUILDING SYSTEM HAS A FEW DIFFERENT WAYS TO MEASURE DISTANCE. WE'LL USUALLY MEASURE PIECES IN TERMS OF THEIR WIDTH AND THEIR HEIGHT. THE LEGO BRICK ON THE RIGHT IS 2 STUDS WIDE AND 1 BRICK HIGH. THREE PLATES ARE EQUAL IN HEIGHT TO ONE BRICK.

2 STUDS WIDE

1 PLATE TALL

3 PLATES = 1 BRICK

A LOT OF BUILDERS KNOW THAT. BUT THERE'S A TOP-SECRET MAGIC FORMULA THAT ONLY EXPERT BUILDERS KNOW:

SO WHAT DOES THIS IMPLY?

2 STUDS

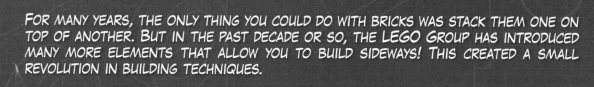

5 PLATES

5 PLATES = 2 STUDS

FOR MANY YEARS, THE ONLY THING YOU COULD DO WITH BRICKS WAS STACK THEM ONE ON TOP OF ANOTHER. BUT IN THE PAST DECADE OR SO, THE LEGO GROUP HAS INTRODUCED MANY MORE ELEMENTS THAT ALLOW YOU TO BUILD SIDEWAYS! THIS CREATED A SMALL REVOLUTION IN BUILDING TECHNIQUES.

WITH THESE SIMPLE BRICKS, YOU CAN LITERALLY BUILD IN A NEW DIMENSION!

IT MIGHT NOT BE OBVIOUS, BUT ALL OF THESE COMBINATIONS WERE BUILT WITH THE MAGIC FORMULA IN MIND. TAKE A CLOSER LOOK. DO YOU SEE HOW THEY'VE BEEN COMBINED?

BUT WAIT, THERE'S MORE! HERE'S ANOTHER EXAMPLE OF AN INTRIGUING PIECE. EVER WONDER WHY THE CLIP ISN'T PERFECTLY CENTERED IN THE PLATE?

WHY THIS GAP?

TO FIND OUT, LET'S ADD A FEW MORE PARTS. IT TURNS OUT THAT IT'S ANOTHER CLEVER DECISION, WITH THE MAGIC FORMULA IN MIND AGAIN.

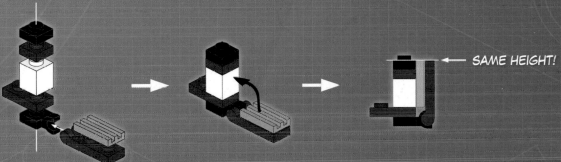

SAME HEIGHT!

THAT'S ALL INTERESTING IN THEORY, BUT HOW CAN WE PUT THIS KNOWLEDGE TO USE? THIS BOOK IS FULL OF EXAMPLES OF THESE TECHNIQUES. HERE ARE A FEW:

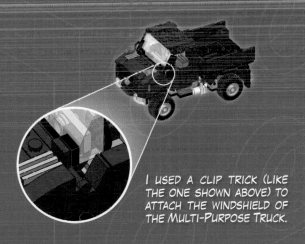

I USED A CLIP TRICK (LIKE THE ONE SHOWN ABOVE) TO ATTACH THE WINDSHIELD OF THE MULTI-PURPOSE TRUCK.

IN THE MUSCLE CAR'S BACK LIGHT, THE MAGIC FORMULA IS CLEARLY VISIBLE!

5 PLATES = 2 STUDS

NOW THAT YOU UNDERSTAND THESE BASIC TECHNIQUES, LET'S START PUTTING THEM INTO PRACTICE.

KEEP YOUR EYES OPEN FOR THE MAGIC FORMULA!

ONE MORE THING! YOU'LL SEE A CLASSIFICATION LIKE THIS ON THE INTRODUCTION PAGE FOR EACH MODEL. THIS TELLS YOU HOW COMPLEX THE MODEL IS.

HOW DIFFICULT THE MODEL IS TO BUILD

HOW MANY WORKING FUNCTIONS IT HAS

HOW MANY PIECES ARE NEEDED

Complexity
Functions
Pieces

LET'S GO!

Complexity

Functions

Pieces

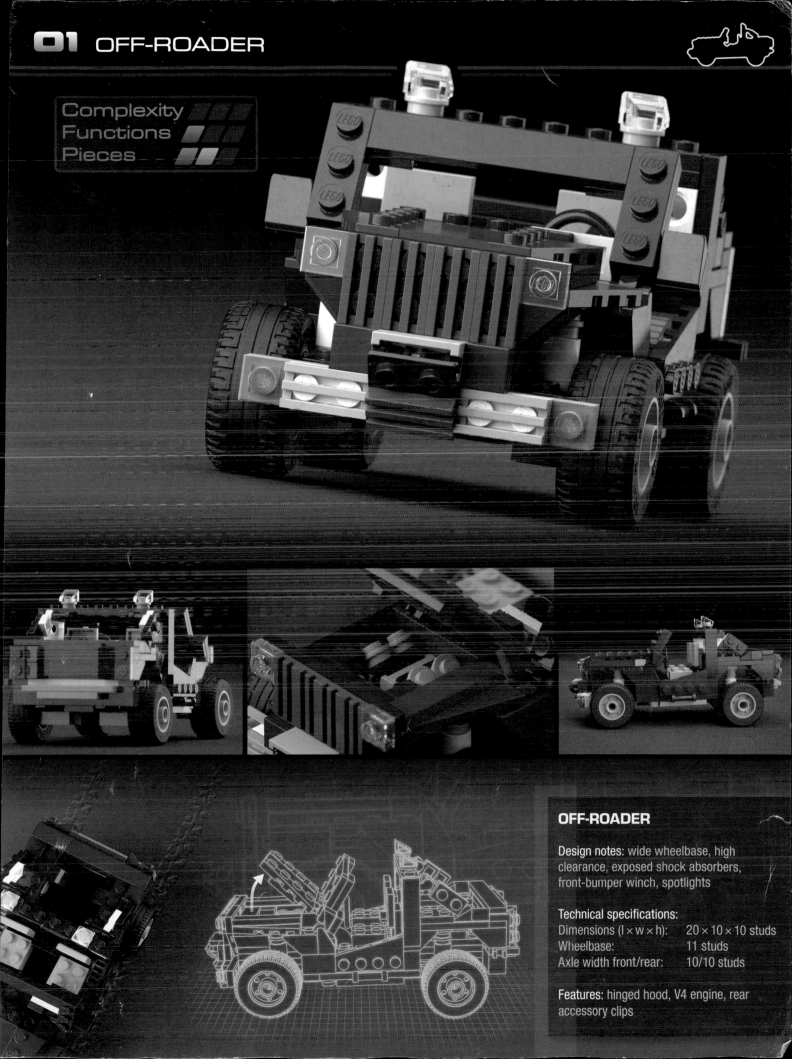

OFF-ROADER

Design notes: wide wheelbase, high clearance, exposed shock absorbers, front-bumper winch, spotlights

Technical specifications:

Dimensions (l × w × h):	20 × 10 × 10 studs
Wheelbase:	11 studs
Axle width front/rear:	10/10 studs

Features: hinged hood, V4 engine, rear accessory clips

1

2x

1x

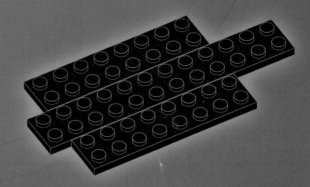

2

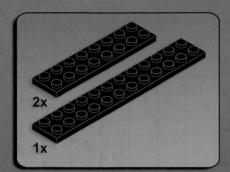

1x   2x

1x

2x

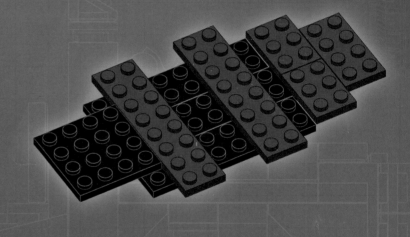

3

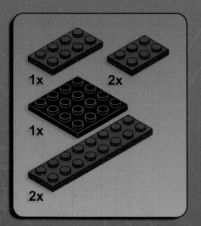

2x   2x

2x

2x   1x

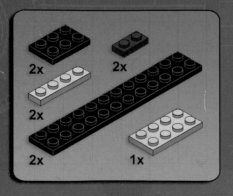

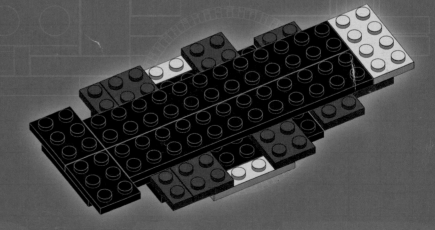

4

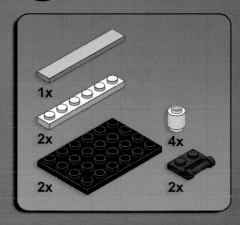

1x
2x
2x
4x
2x

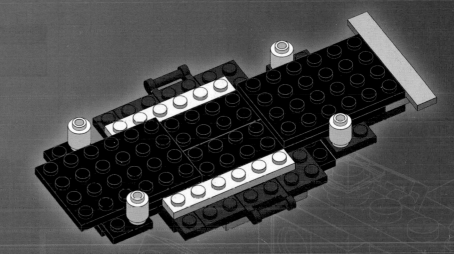

5

2x
1x
1x
1x
2x
2x
2x

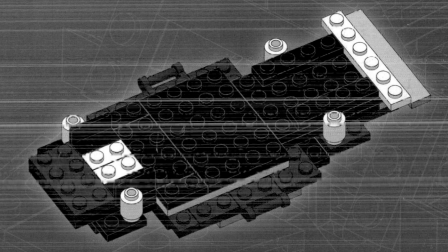

6

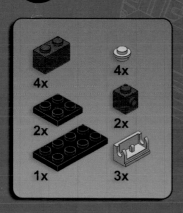

4x
4x
2x
2x
1x
3x

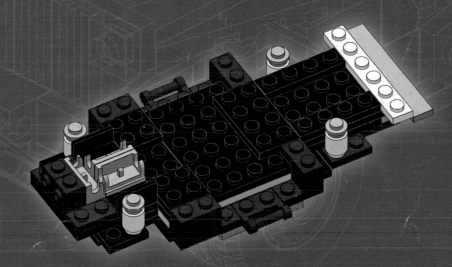

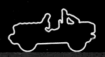

7

2x

4x 4x 1x

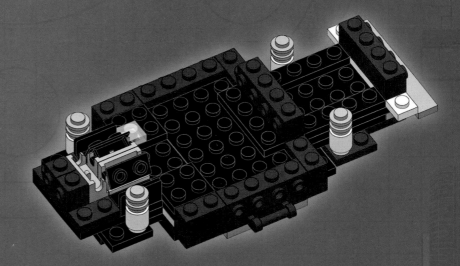

8

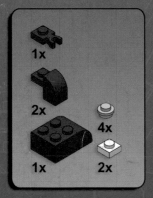

1x

2x

4x

1x 2x

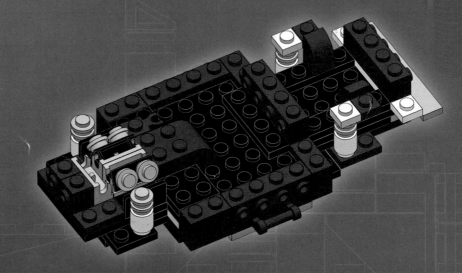

9

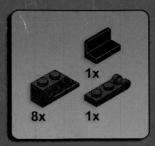

1x

8x 1x

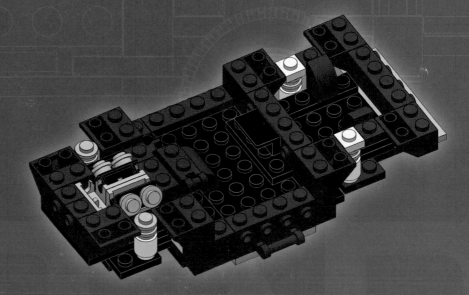

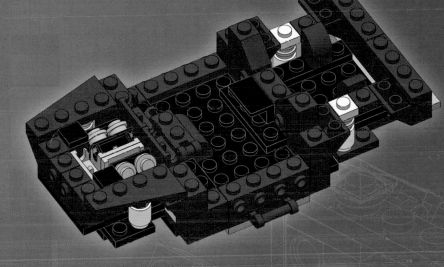

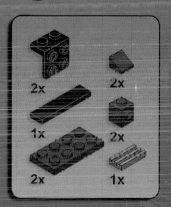

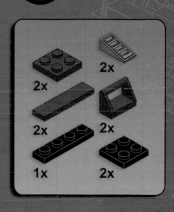

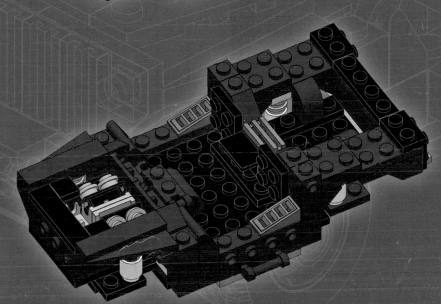

13

2x

2x

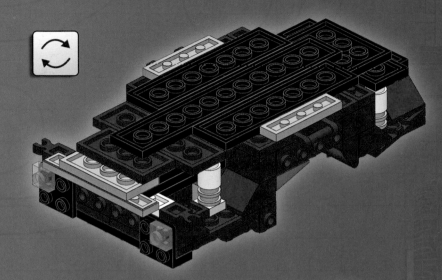

14

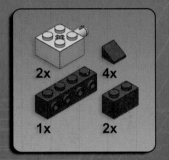

2x 4x

1x 2x

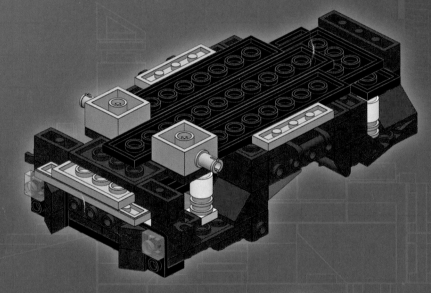

15

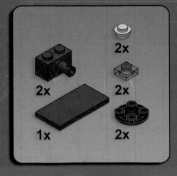

2x

2x 2x

1x 2x

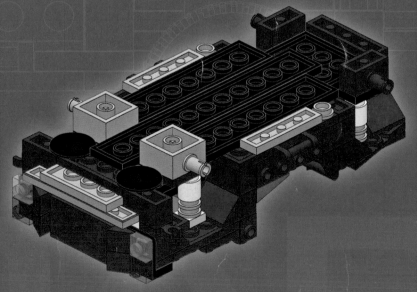

16

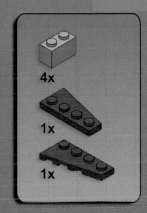

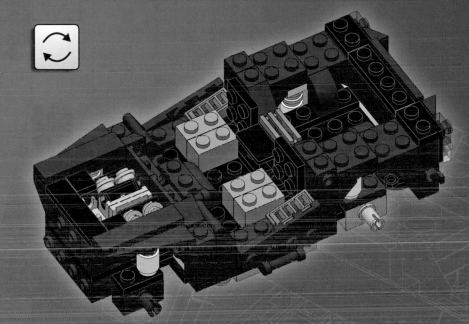

17

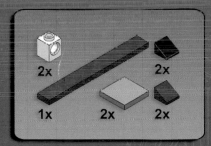

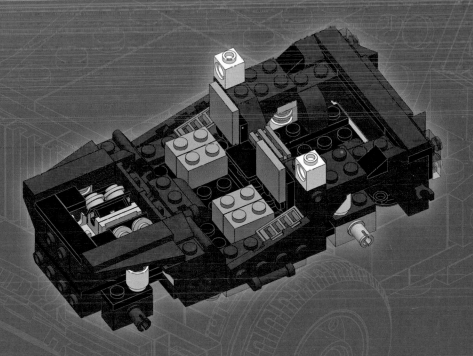

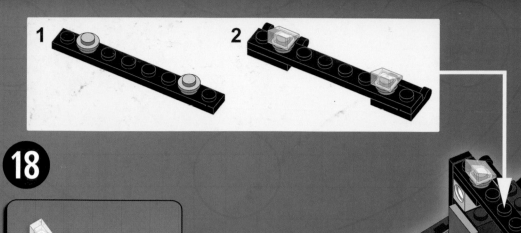

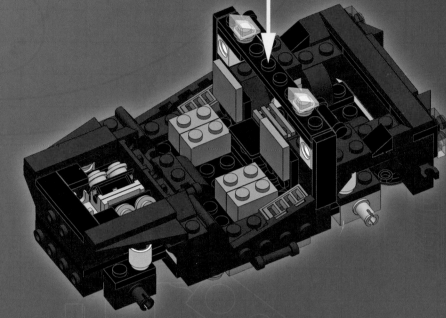

18

19

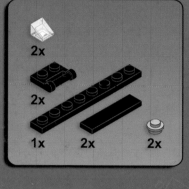

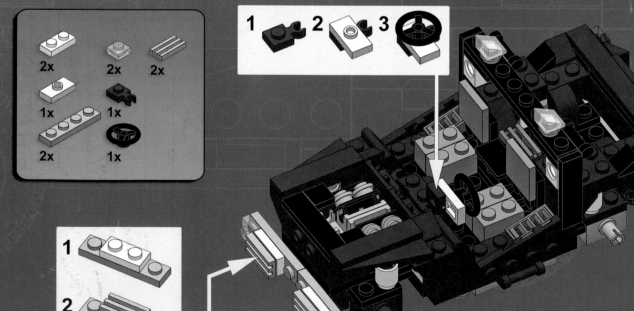

20

1
2

1x
2x
1x
1x
1x
1x

21

2x
2x
1x
2x
1x
1x
5x

1
2
3

1   **2**   **3**

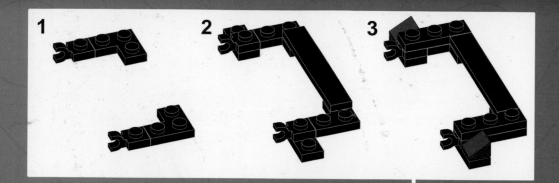

22

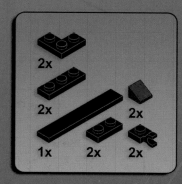

2x
2x   2x
1x   2x   2x

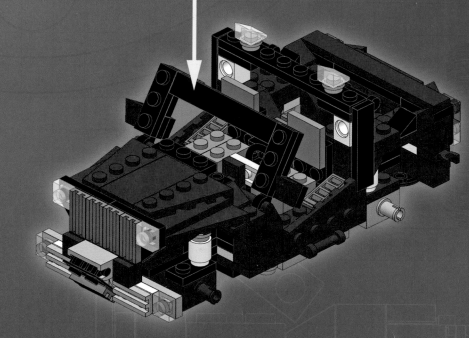

23

4x
2x
4x   2x

x2

Complexity
Functions
Pieces

GO-KART

Design notes: wide and low chassis, single-cylinder engine, large seat, small wheels, gas and brake pedals

Technical specifications:
Dimensions (l × w × h):   21 × 12 × 9 studs
Wheelbase: 14 studs
Axle width front/rear: 12/12 studs

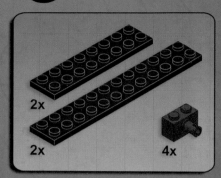

2x

2x

4x

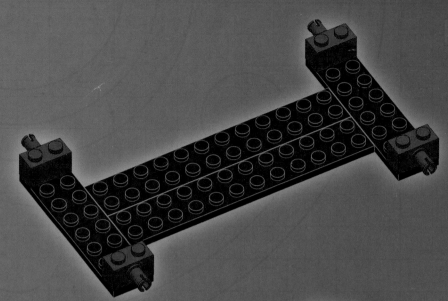

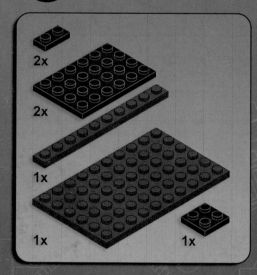

2x

2x

1x

1x

1x

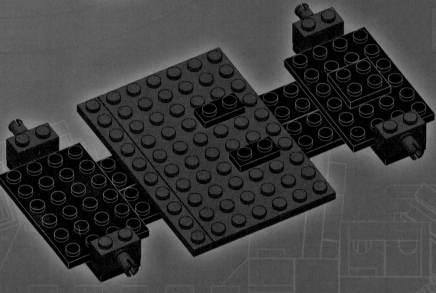

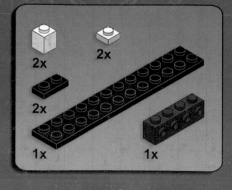

2x

2x

2x

1x

1x

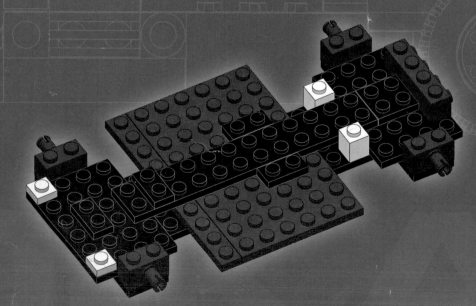

4

2x
2x
2x
2x
1x
4x

5

4x
4x
2x
1x
1x

6

2x
2x
2x

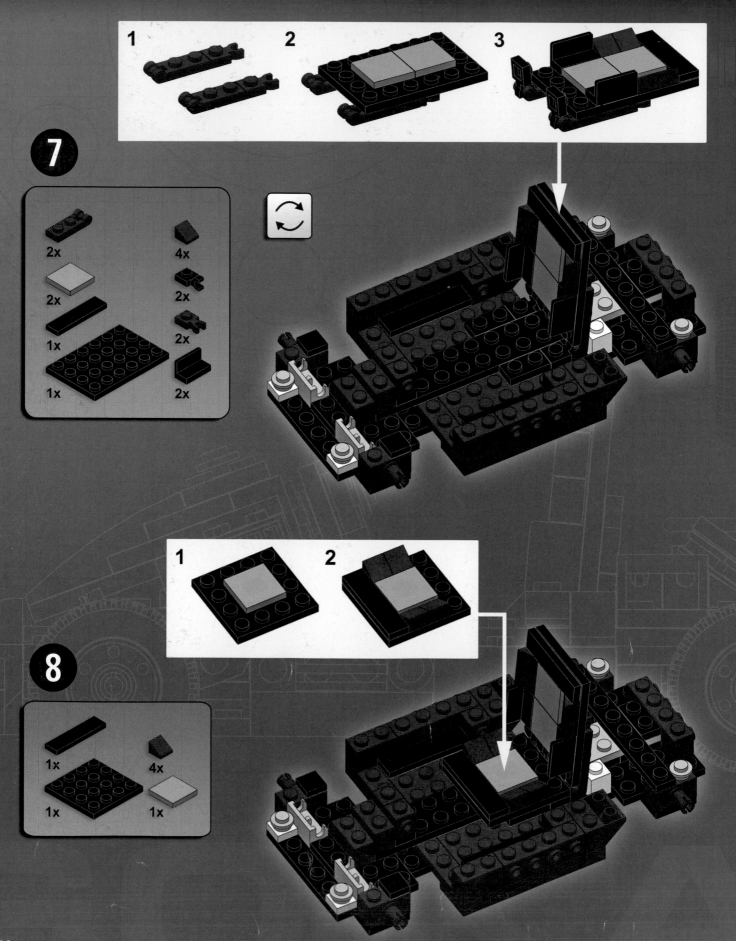

9

2x
1x
2x
1x
2x

10

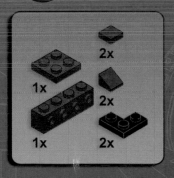

1x
2x
1x
2x
1x
2x

11

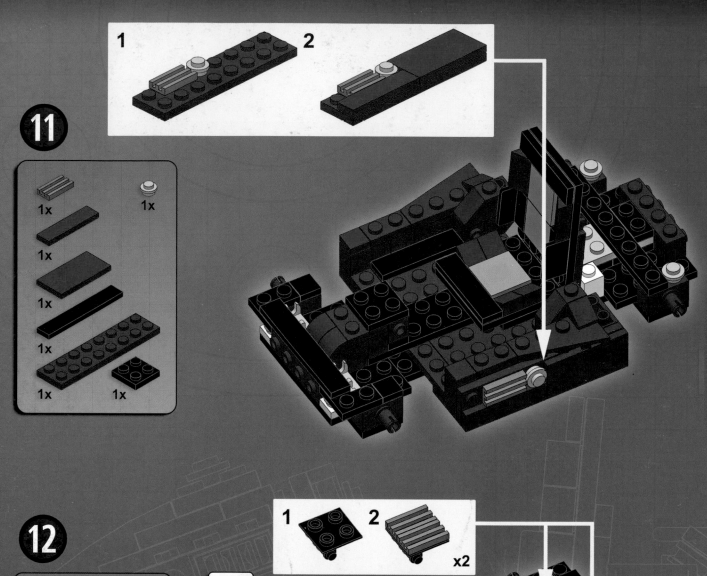

12

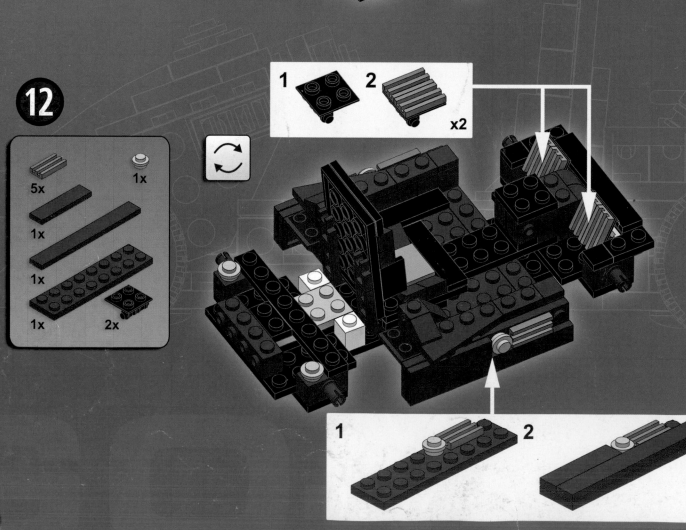

13

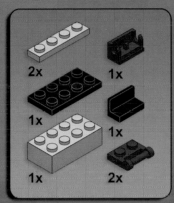

2x   1x
1x   1x
1x   2x

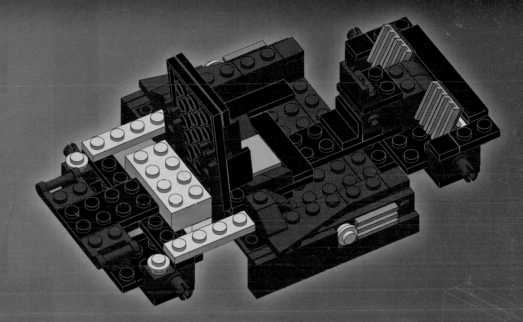

14

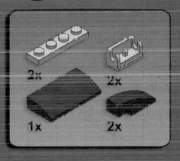

2x   2x
1x   2x

1   2   3

15

1x   2x   4x
1x   1x   1x

16

1   2   3

2x   4x
1x   2x

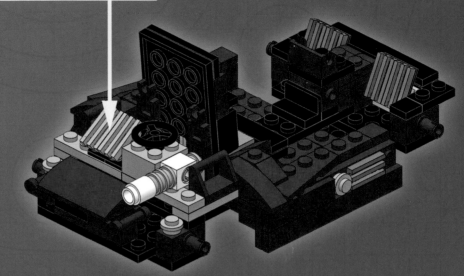

17

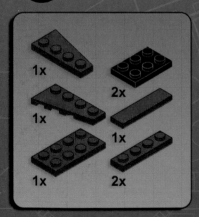

1x
    2x
1x
    1x
1x   2x

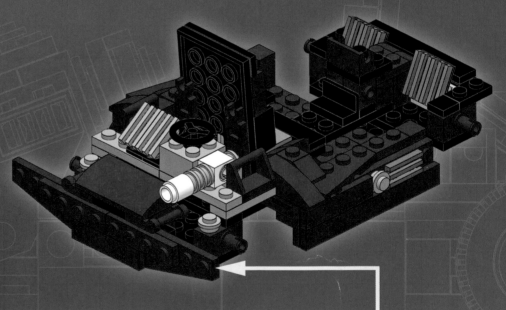

1   2   3

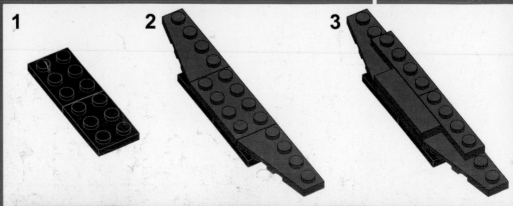

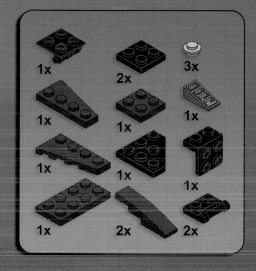

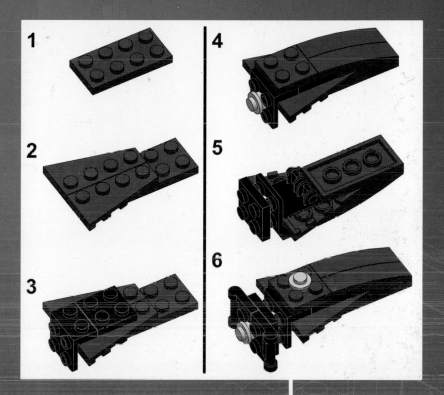

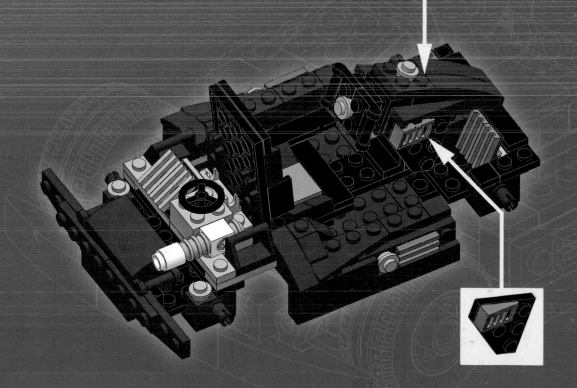

19

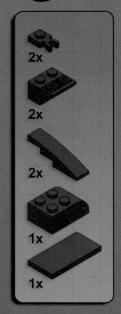

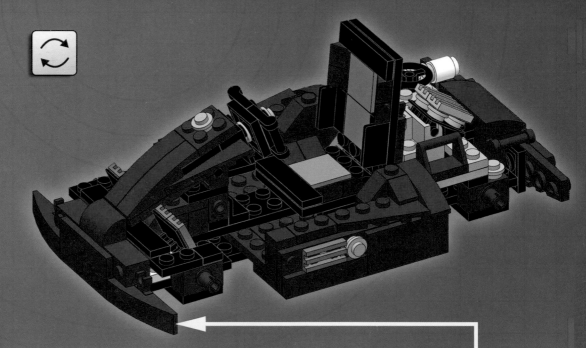

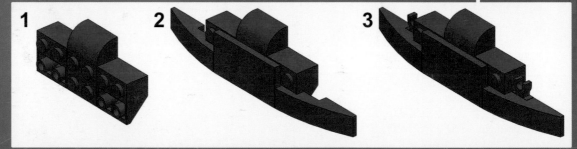

1   2   3

20

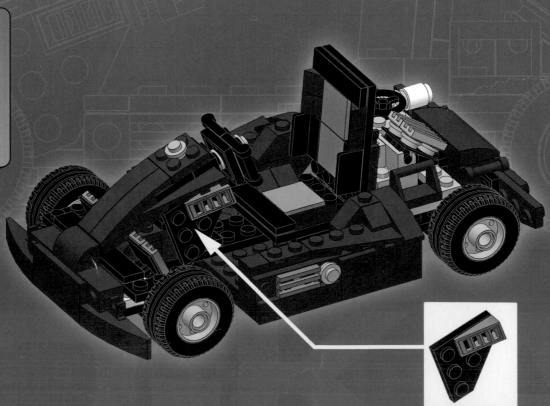

Complexity

Functions

Pieces

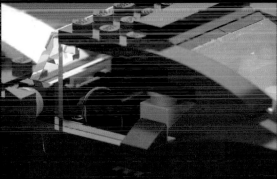

MUSCLE CAR

Design notes: fastback body design, hood scoop, exposed exhaust pipes

Technical specifications:
Dimensions (l × w × h): 21 × 10 × 8 studs
Wheelbase: 12 studs
Axle width front/rear: 8/8 studs

Features: opening doors

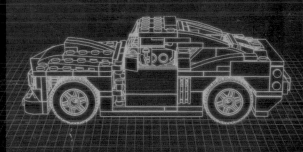

1

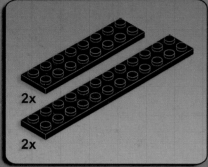

2x

2x

2

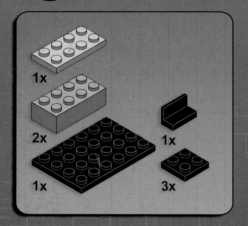

1x

2x

1x

1x

3x

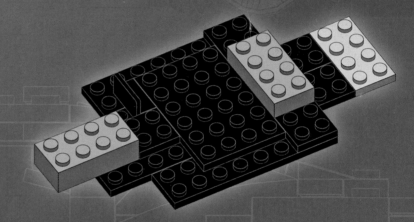

3

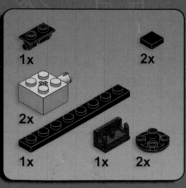

1x

2x

2x

1x

1x

2x

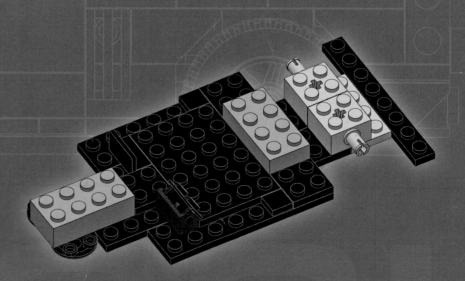

4

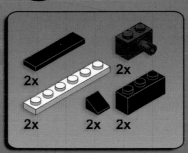

2x 2x
2x 2x 2x

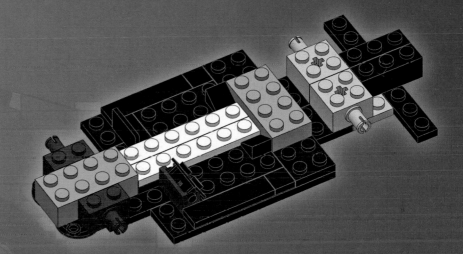

5

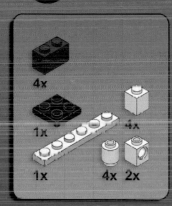

4x
1x 4x
1x 4x 2x

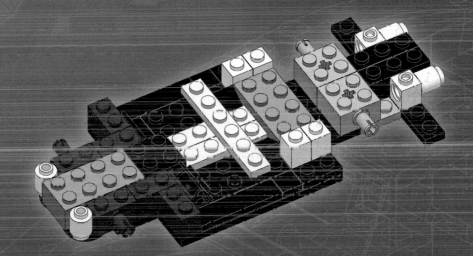

6

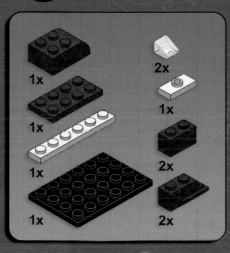

1x 2x
1x 1x
1x 2x
1x 2x

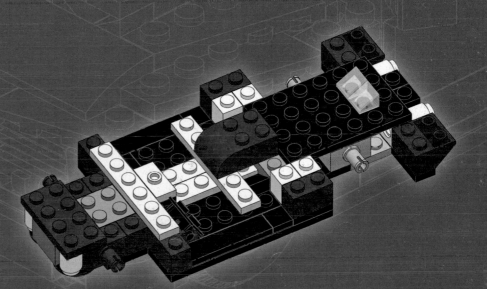

7

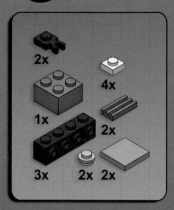

2x
4x
1x
2x
3x 2x 2x

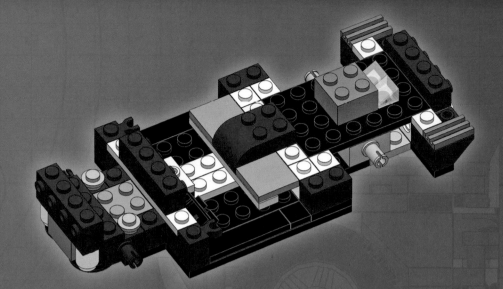

8

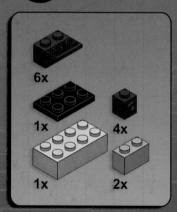

6x
1x 4x
1x 2x

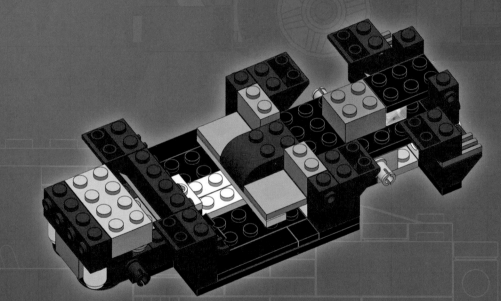

9

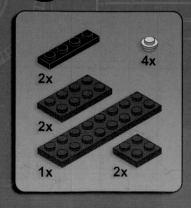

4x
2x
2x
1x 2x

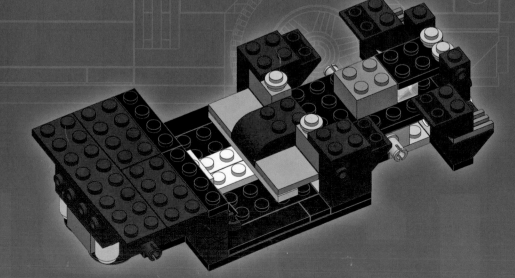

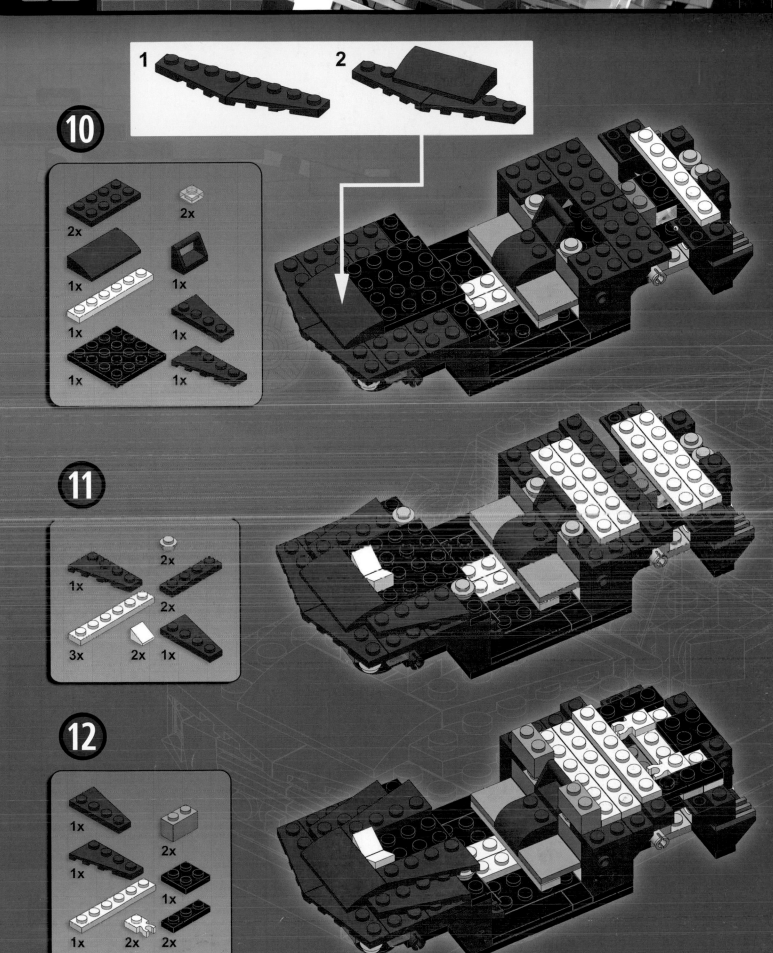

13

2x 1x

2x 2x 1x

14

2x
2x
2x
2x
6x
1x 2x 2x

1 2 3 x2

15

1x
2x 1x
1x 4x 2x

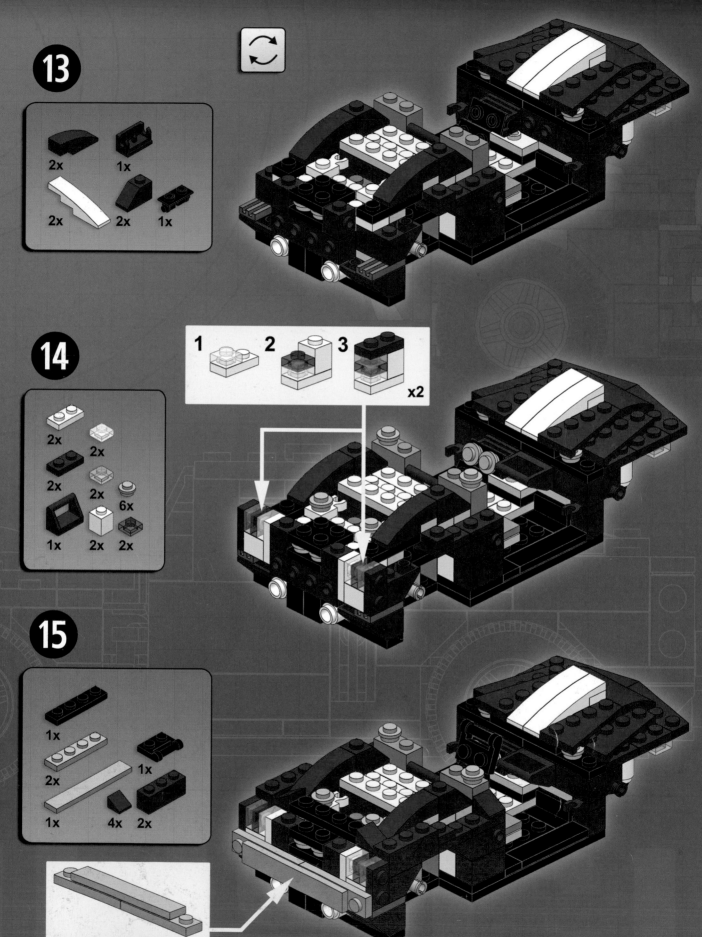

16

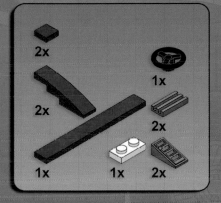

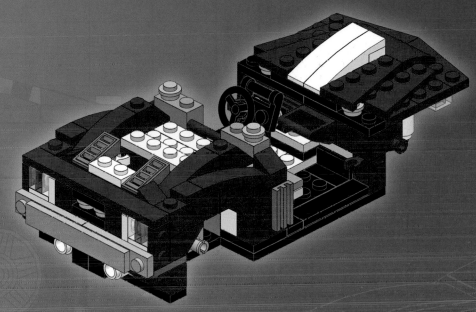

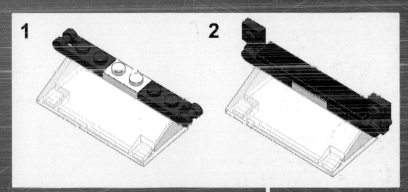

17

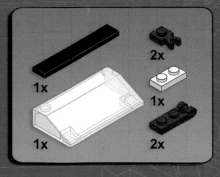

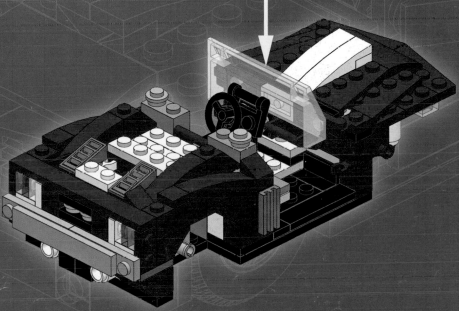

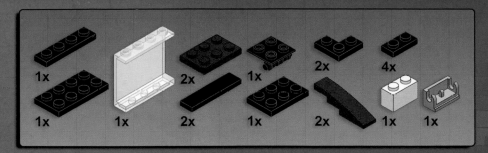

18

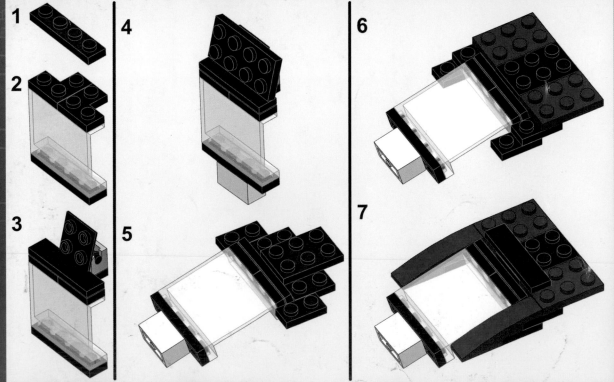

19

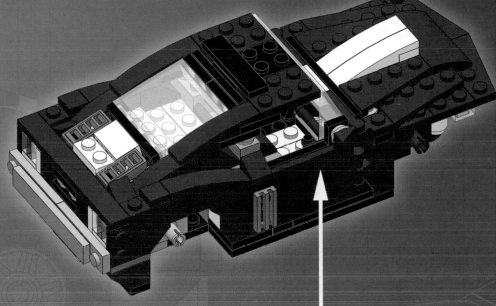

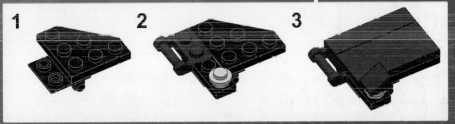

20

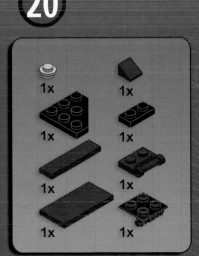

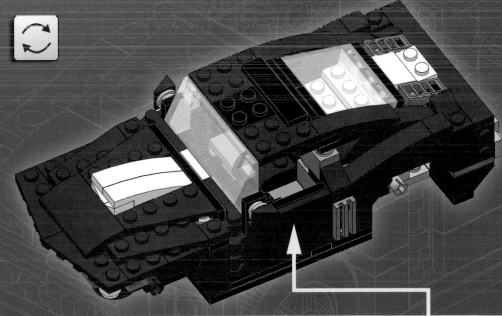

21

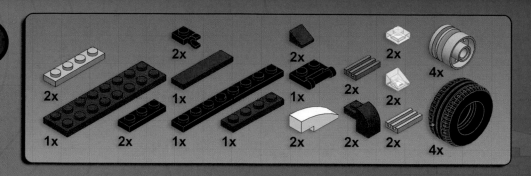

2x 2x 2x 4x

2x 2x 2x

1x 2x 1x 1x 2x 2x 2x 4x

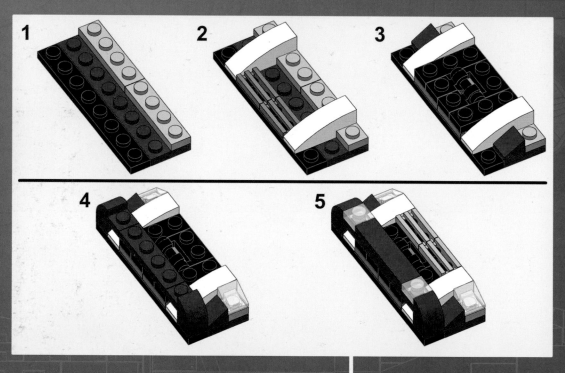

1 2 3

4 5

Complexity
Functions
Pieces

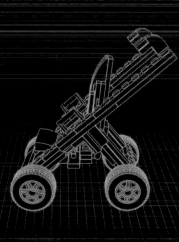

STROLLER

Design notes: open frame, upright chair, curved handlebars

Technical specifications:
Dimensions (l × w × h): 14 × 10 × 15 studs
Wheelbase: 8 studs
Axle width front/rear: 10/10 studs

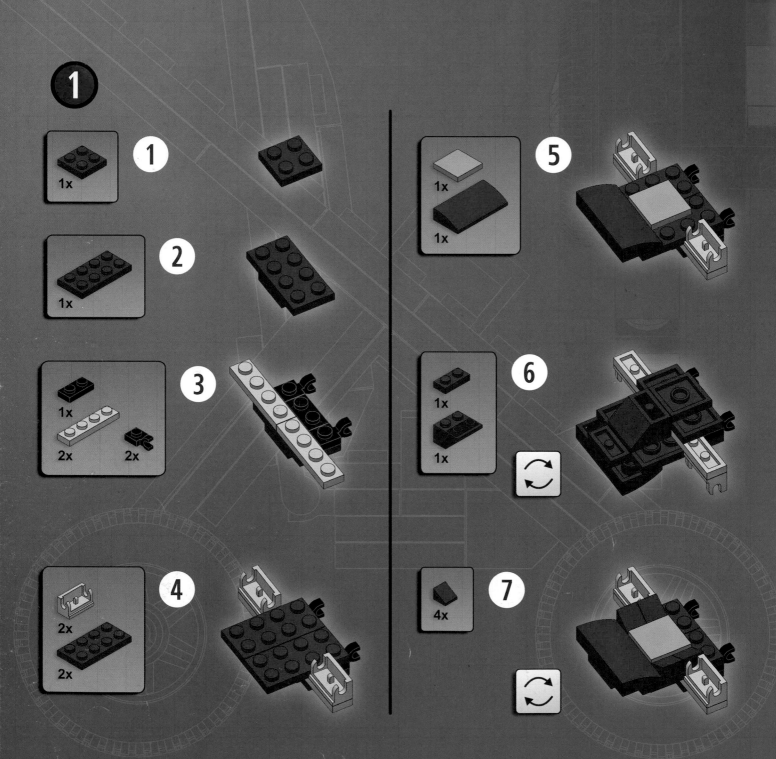

2

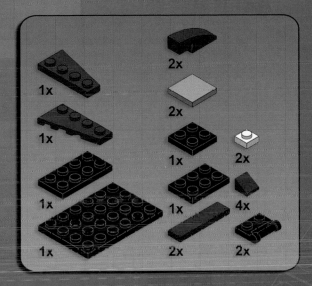

1x 2x 2x 1x 2x 1x 1x 1x 2x 4x 2x

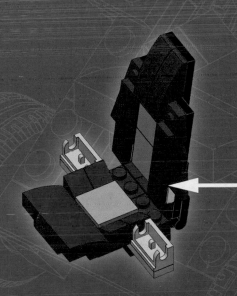

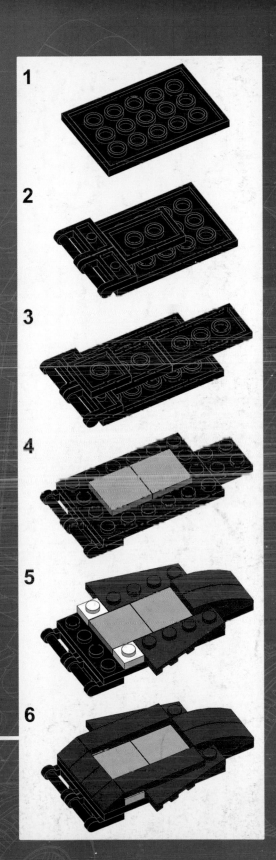

1 2 3 4 5 6

3

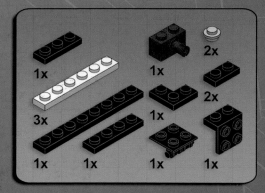

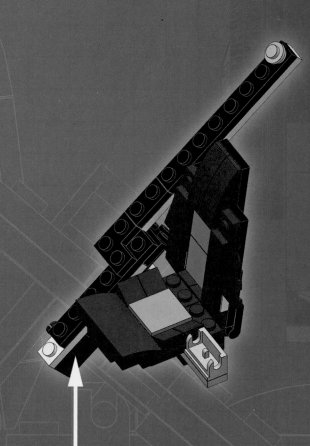

1

2

3

4

5

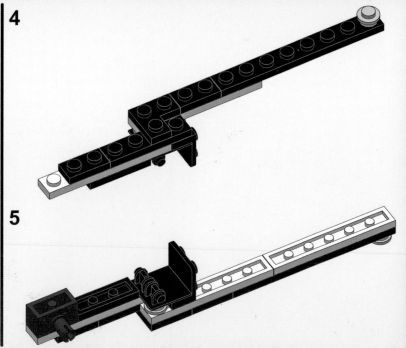

4

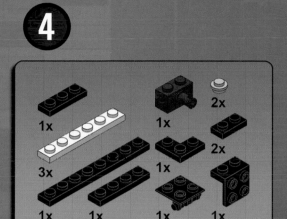

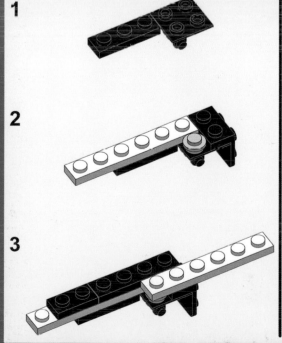

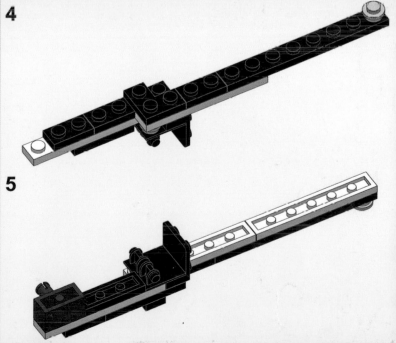

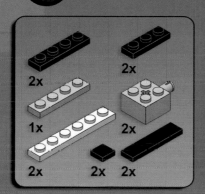

2x
2x
1x
2x
2x 2x 2x

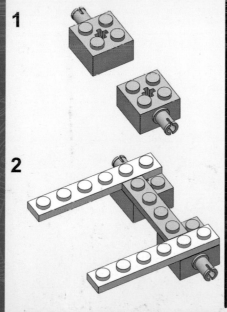

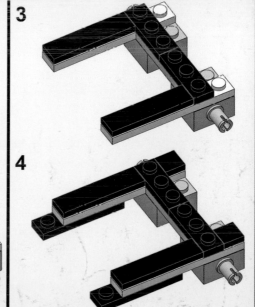

1

2

3

4

7

8

Complexity
Functions
Pieces

MULTI-PURPOSE TRUCK

Design notes: short nose, wide axle, high clearance

Technical specifications:

Dimensions (l × w × h):	19 × 11 × 11 studs
Wheelbase:	11 studs
Axle width front/rear:	10/10 studs

Features: tipping bed

1

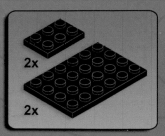

2x

2x

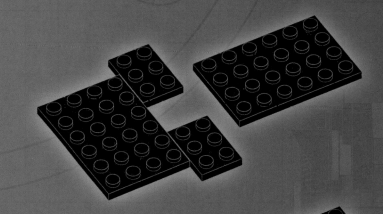

2

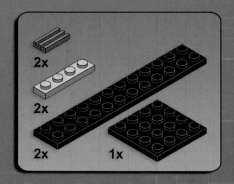

2x

2x

2x   1x

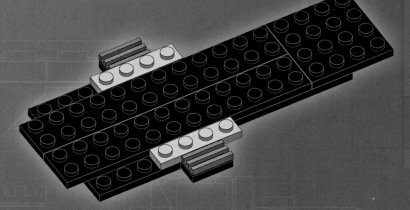

3

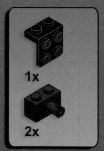

1x

2x

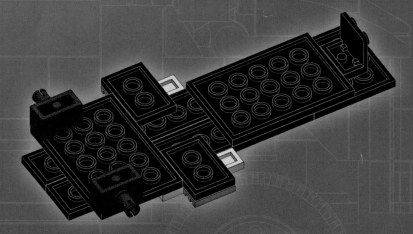

4

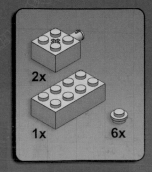

2x

1x   6x

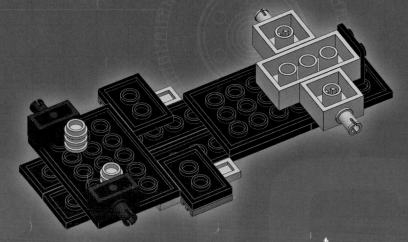

5

2x
1x 1x

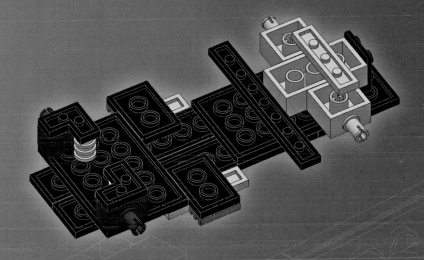

6

1x 2x
1x 2x 1x

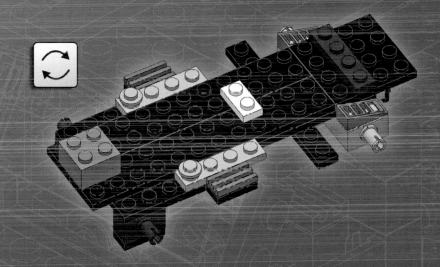

7

3x 2x
1x 1x
1x 3x

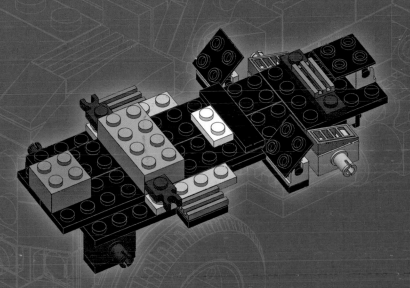

8

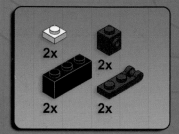

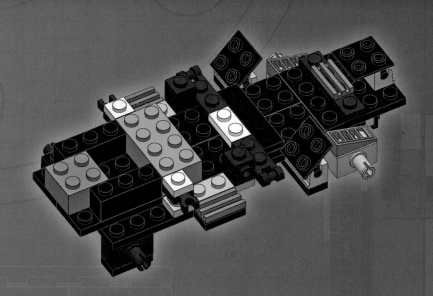

9

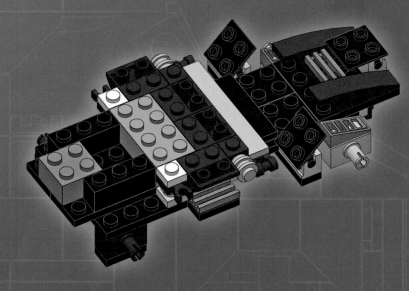

10

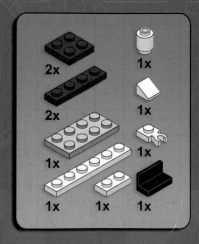

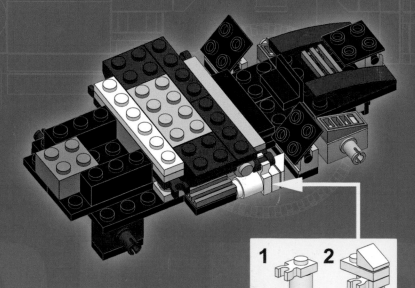

11

2x

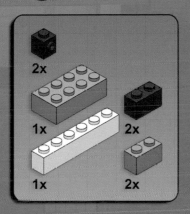
1x   2x

1x   2x

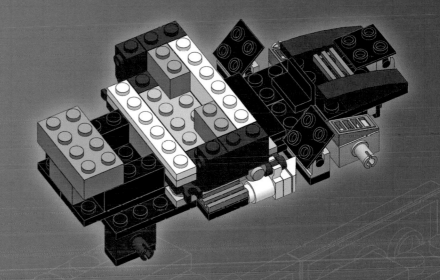

12

2x   2x

2x

1x   1x

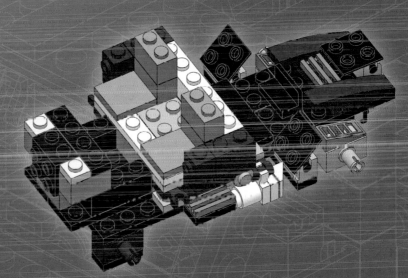

13

2x   2x

1x   2x

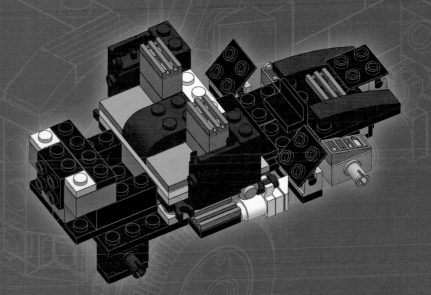

14

1x 1x
1x 1x

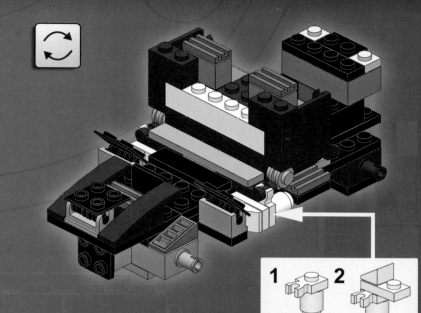

1 2

15

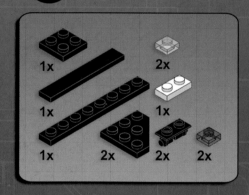

1x
1x 2x
1x 1x
1x 2x 2x 2x

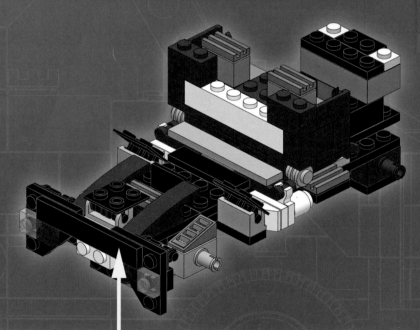

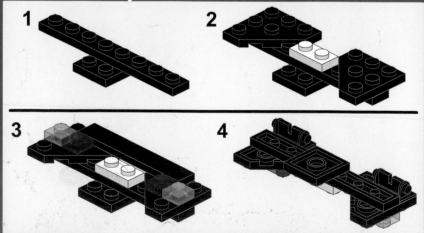

1 2

3 4

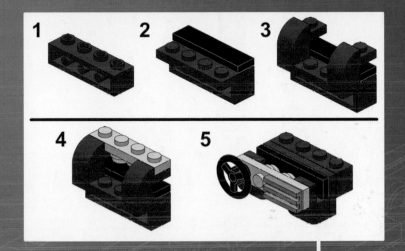

16

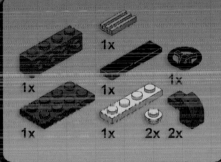

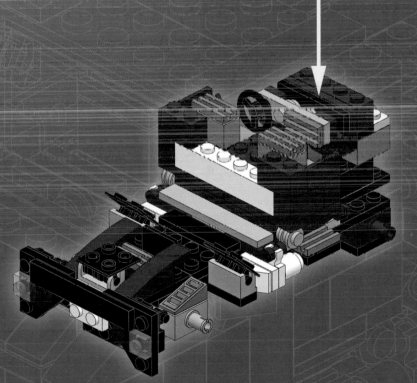

17

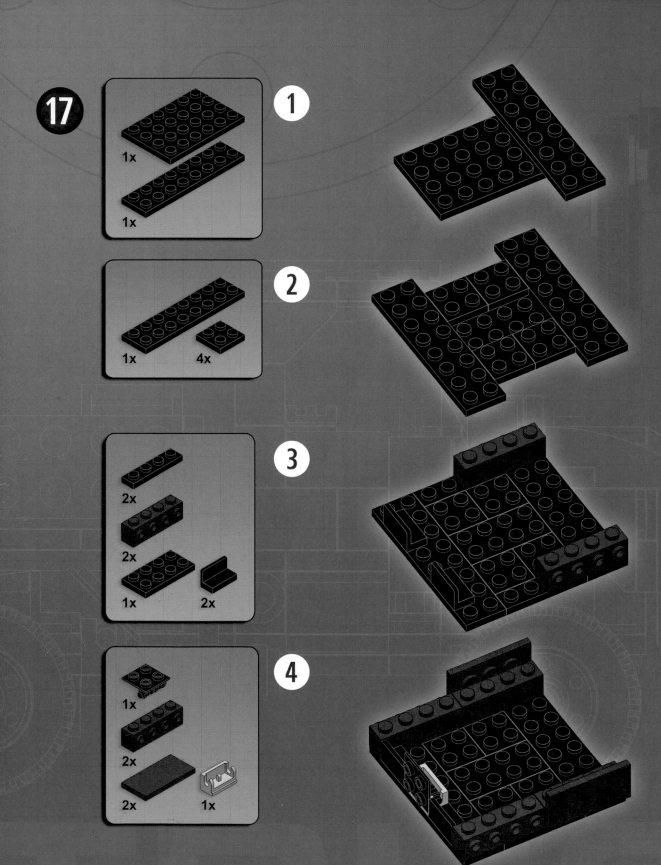

1

1x

1x

2

1x   4x

3

2x

2x

1x   2x

4

1x

2x

2x   1x

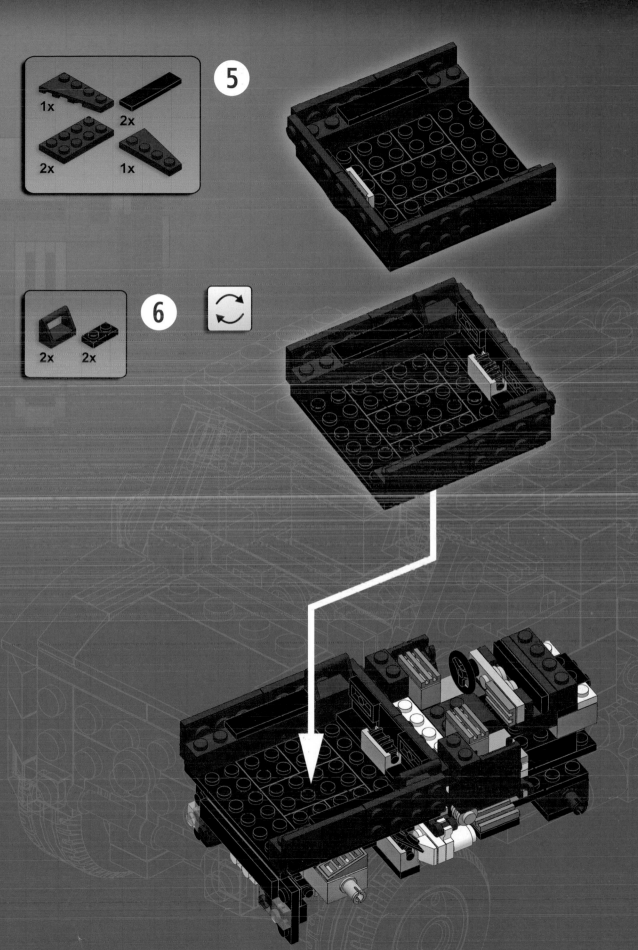

5

1x 2x
2x 1x

6

2x 2x

18

1
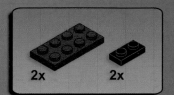
2x 2x

2

2x 2x
1x 2x

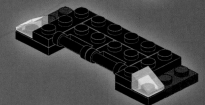

3
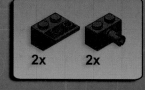
2x 2x

4
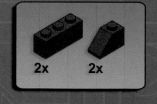
2x 2x

5

2x 2x

6

6x 2x 1x

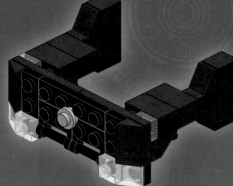

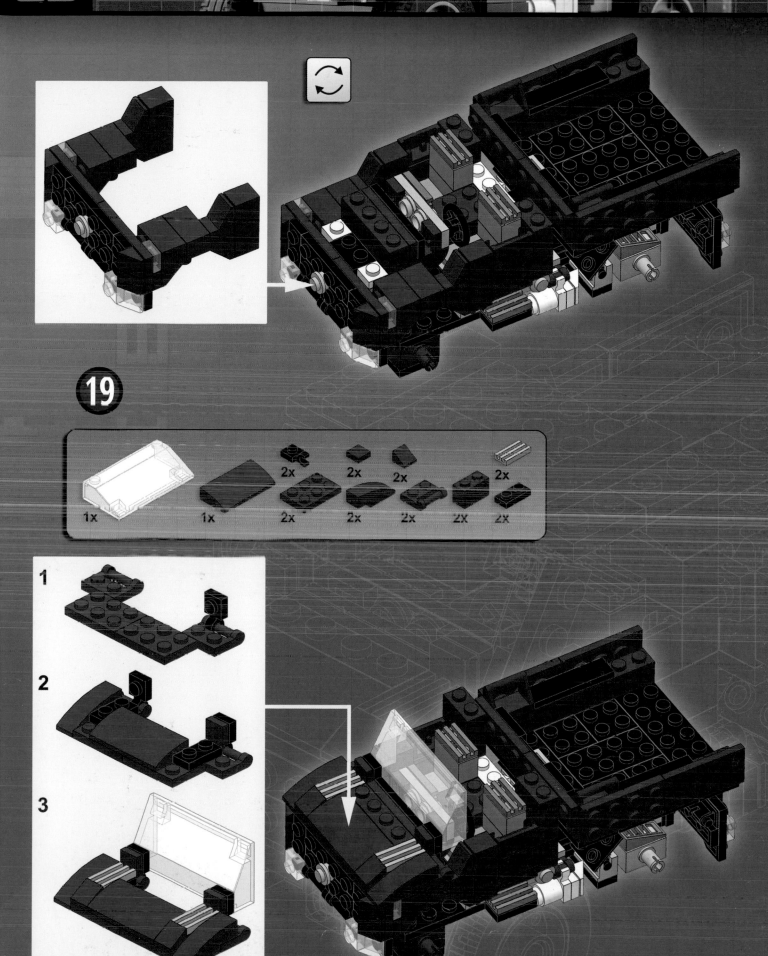

19

1

2

3

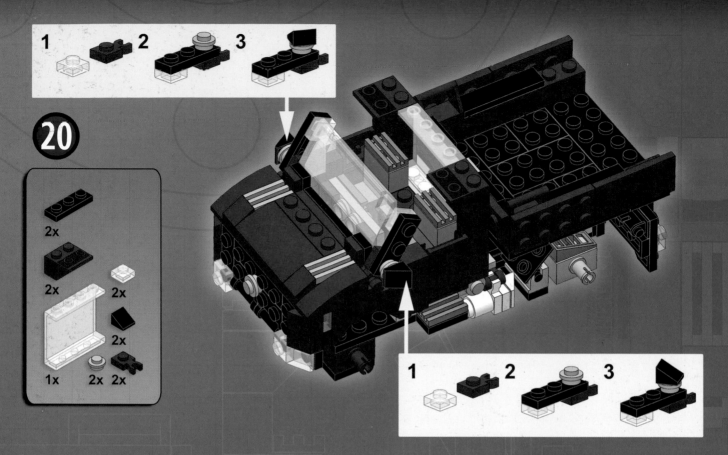

20

21

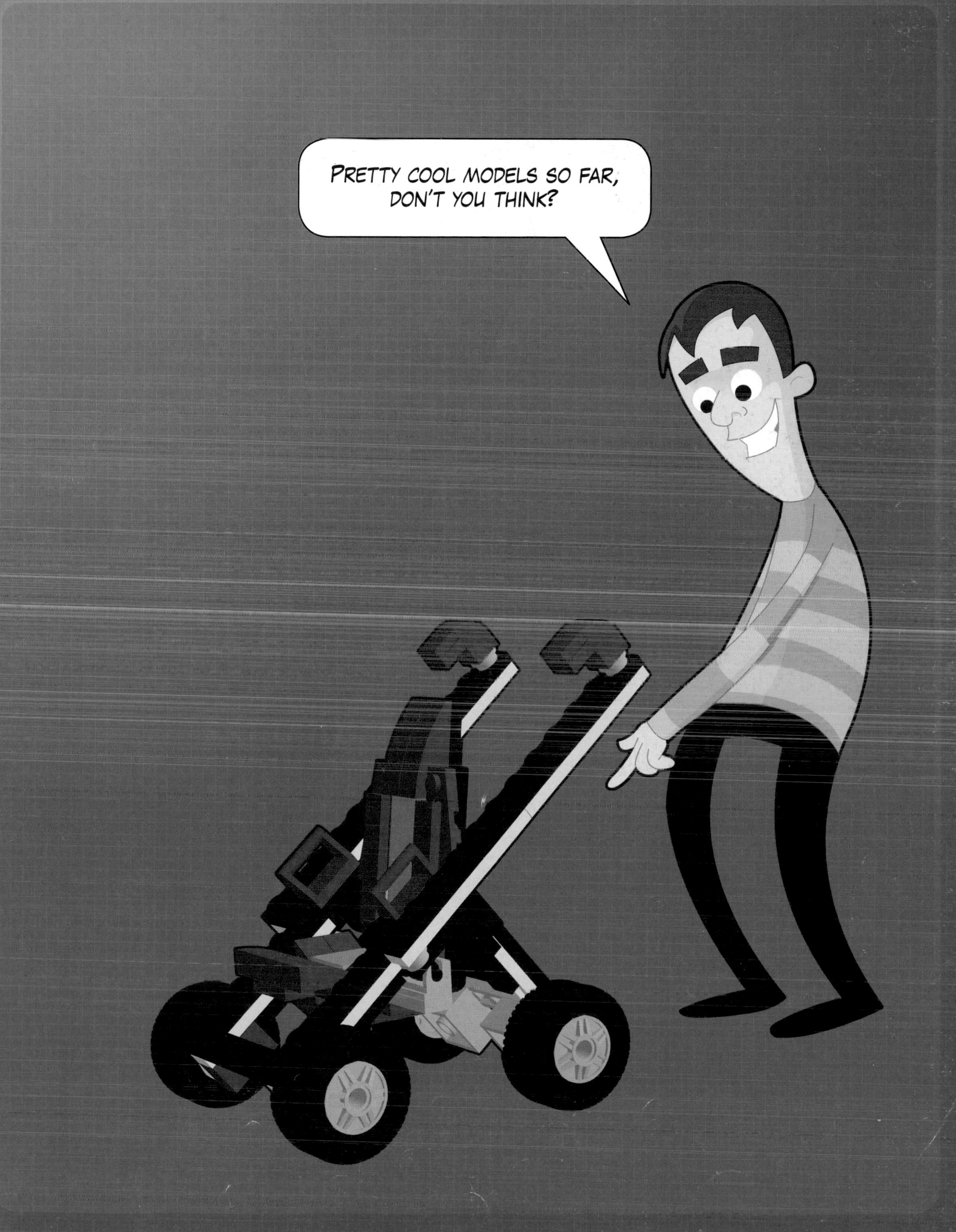
PRETTY COOL MODELS SO FAR, DON'T YOU THINK?

ADVANCED BUILDING

Now you're ready to learn some advanced building techniques!

Here are a few ideas for creating sturdy cross-connections between pieces.

That's a **STRONG CONNECTION!**

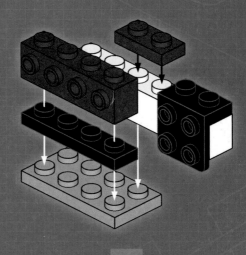

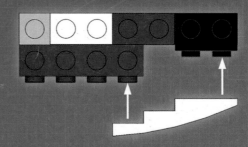

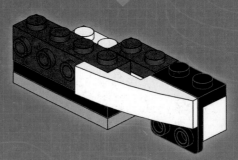

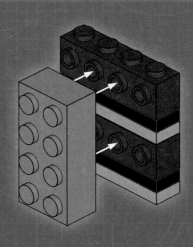

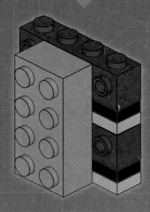

VERTICAL REINFORCEMENT

HORIZONTAL REINFORCEMENT

WHAT HAPPENS WHEN YOU BUILD SIDEWAYS AFTER YOU'VE ALREADY GONE SIDEWAYS? WELL, THEN YOU'RE BUILDING UPSIDE DOWN!

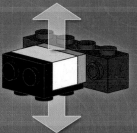

DON'T GET DISORIENTED!

OR YOU MIGHT BE BUILDING RIGHT SIDE UP AGAIN, TOO!

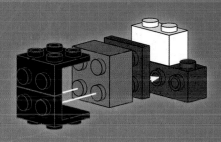

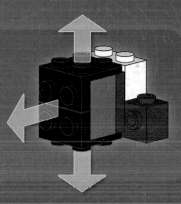

NOTICE HOW YOU CAN REINFORCE THIS CONNECTION WITH A PLATE OR BRICK ON THE TOP.

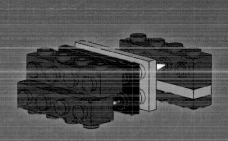

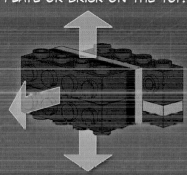

ANOTHER SURPRISINGLY USEFUL TECHNIQUE IS TO USE HINGES TO BUILD SIDEWAYS. THESE HINGES CAN BE HELPFUL WHEN YOU'RE OUT OF THE USUAL PARTS FOR BUILDING SIDEWAYS, AND THEY'RE EVEN PREFERABLE WHEN YOU WANT TO BUILD AT OTHER ANGLES.

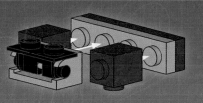

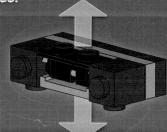

UPSIDE-DOWN BUILDING IS COOL!

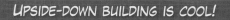

UPSIDE-DOWN BUILDING WITH THE MAGIC FORMULA

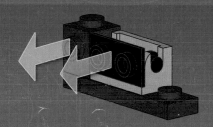

HINGES AND PINS ARE VERY USEFUL FOR CREATING FLEXIBLE JOINTS AND ARTICULATION. DIFFERENT HINGES HAVE DIFFERENT LIMITATIONS, THOUGH.

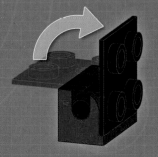

90° RANGE

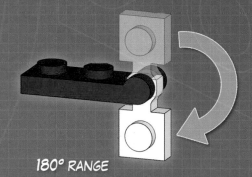

180° RANGE

360° RANGE

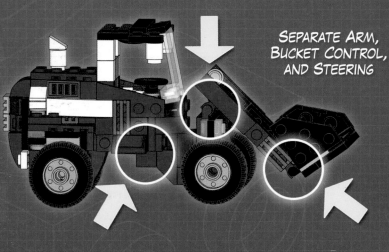

SEPARATE ARM, BUCKET CONTROL, AND STEERING

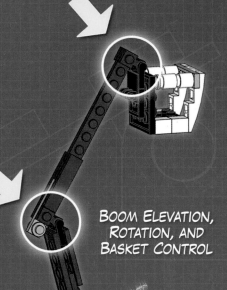

BOOM ELEVATION, ROTATION, AND BASKET CONTROL

FOR EVERY DIFFERENT KIND OF JOINT, THERE'S AN IDEAL HINGE TO USE. COMBINE THESE JOINTS WITH SIDEWAYS BUILDING TECHNIQUES, AND YOU CAN CREATE PRETTY MUCH ANY FUNCTION OR ARTICULATION! HERE ARE A FEW EXAMPLES I USED IN THIS BOOK.

HINGED DOOR

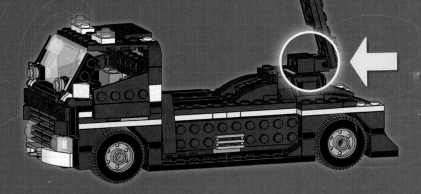

PAY ATTENTION TO THESE TECHNIQUES AS YOU BUILD THE WHEEL LOADER, CLASSIC CAR, AND RESCUE TRUCK!

Complexity

Functions

Pieces

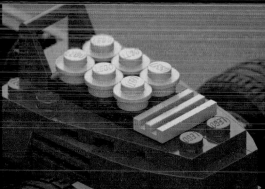

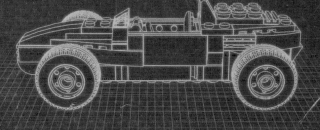

HISTORIC RACER

Design notes: bullet shape, minimal aeroscreen, wide wheelbase, six-cylinder engine, rollbar

Technical specifications:
Dimensions (l × w × h):	19 × 10 × 6 studs
Wheelbase:	12 studs
Axle width front/rear:	10/10 studs

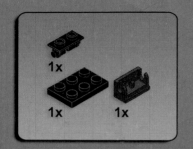

1x
1x 1x

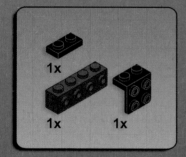

1x
1x 1x

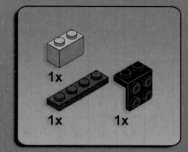

1x
1x 1x

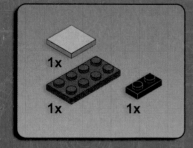

1x
1x 1x

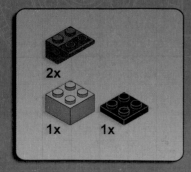

2x
1x 1x

6

2x
1x
2x

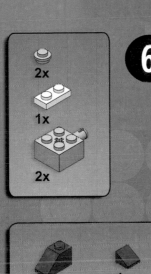

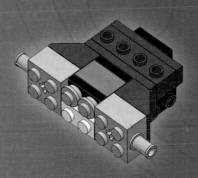

7

2x
1x
1x
1x

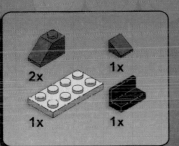

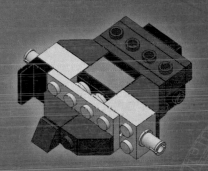

8

1x
2x
1x
1x

9

2x
1x

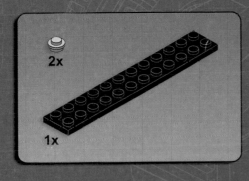

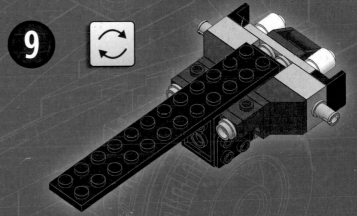

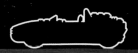

10

1

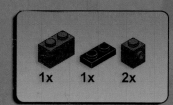

1x 1x 2x

2

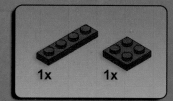

1x 1x

3

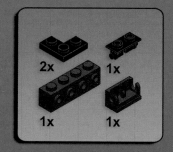

2x 1x

1x 1x

4

1x

1x 2x

5

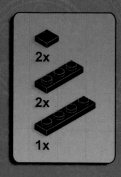

2x

2x

1x

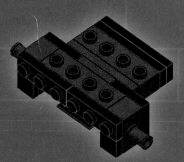

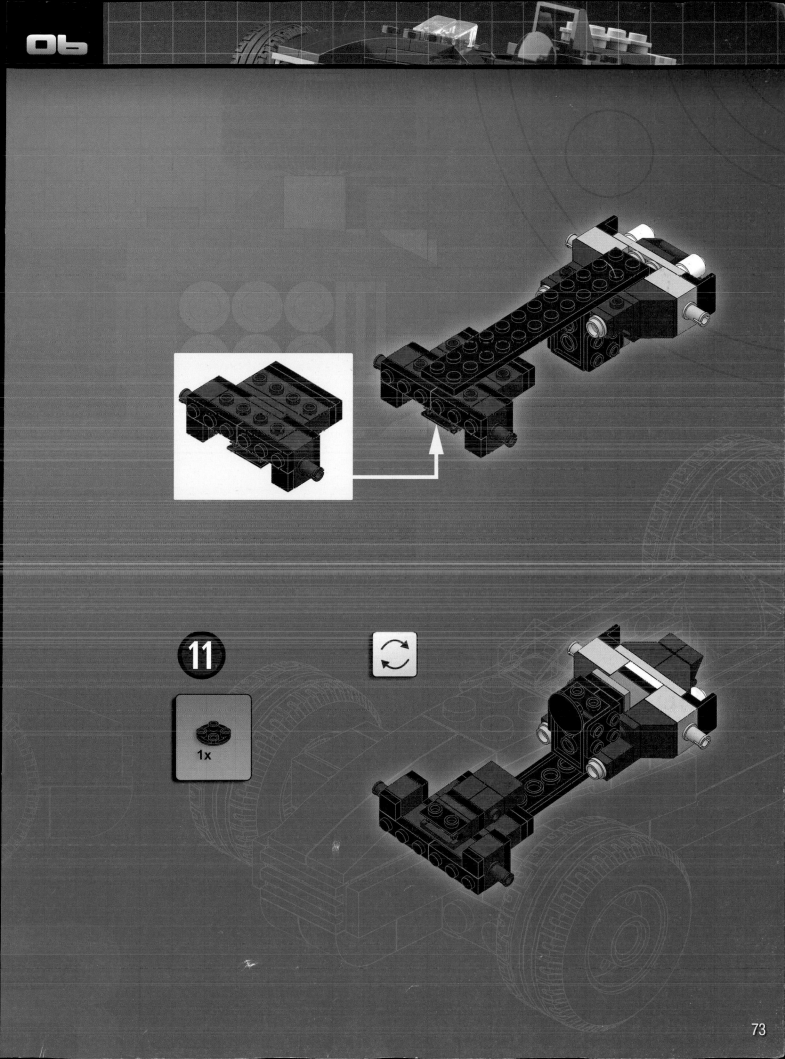

11

1x

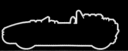

12

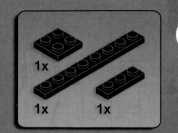

1x
1x 1x

1

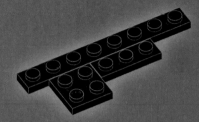

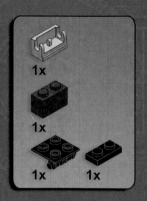

1x
1x 1x
1x 1x

2

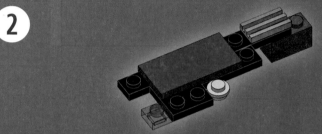

2x
1x
1x 1x

3

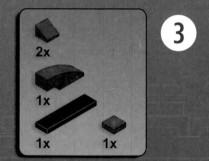

1x
1x
1x 1x

4

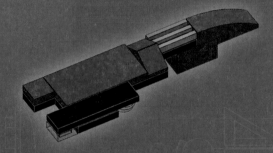

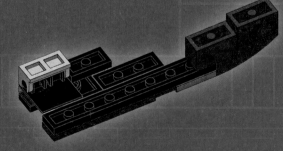

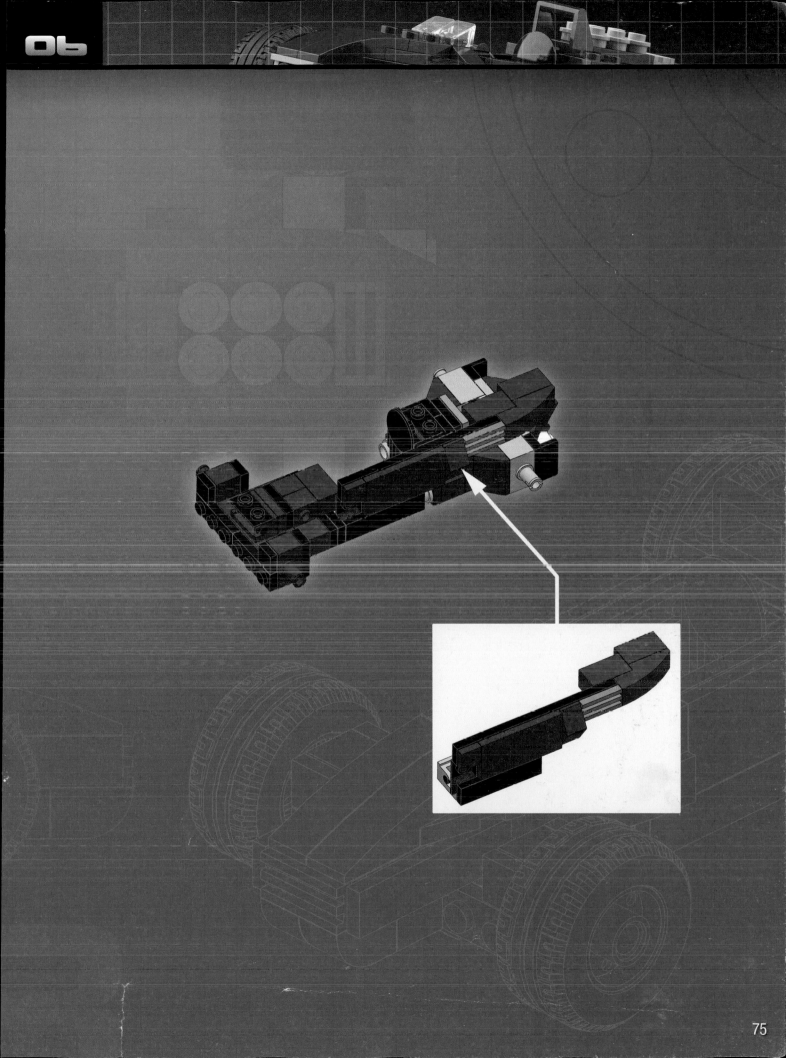

13

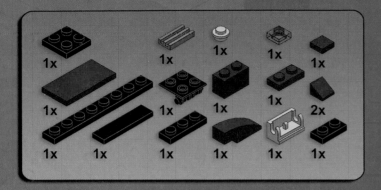

1x 1x 1x 1x 1x
1x 1x 1x 1x 2x
1x 1x 1x 1x 1x 1x

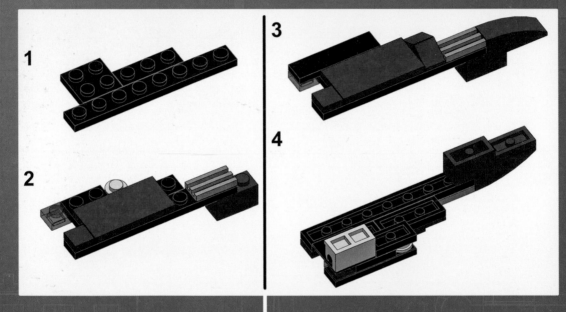

1

2

3

4

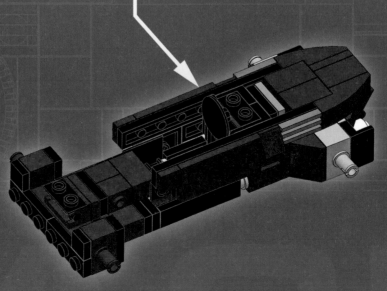

14

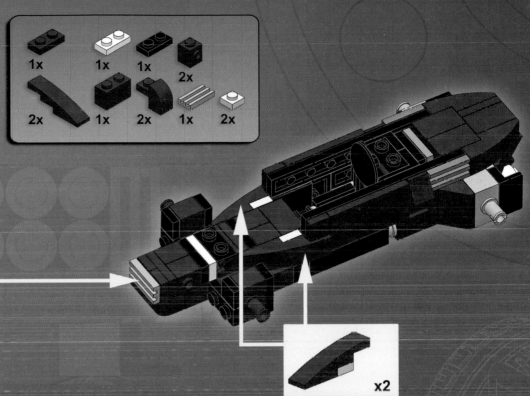

1
2
3
4

1x 1x 1x 2x
2x 1x 2x 1x 2x

x2

15

1 2 3

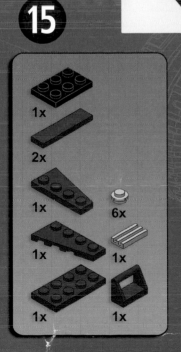

1x
2x
1x 6x
1x 1x
1x 1x

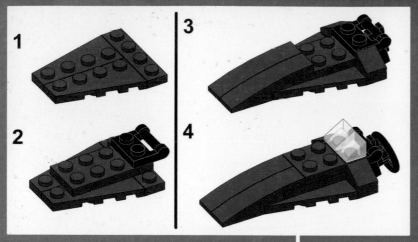

16

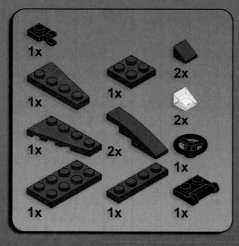

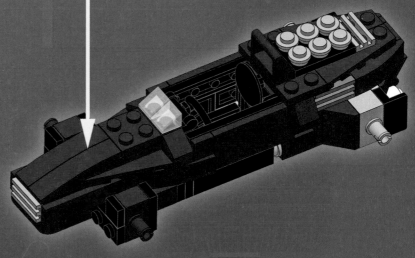

17

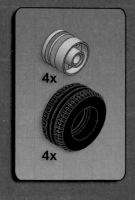

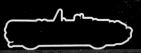

Complexity
Functions
Pieces

CLASSIC CAR

Design notes: wide chassis, convertible, wide stripe, classic curves

Technical specifications:
Dimensions (l × w × h): 23 × 13 × 7 studs
Wheelbase: 12 studs
Axle width front/rear: 10/10 studs

Features: opening doors

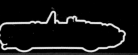

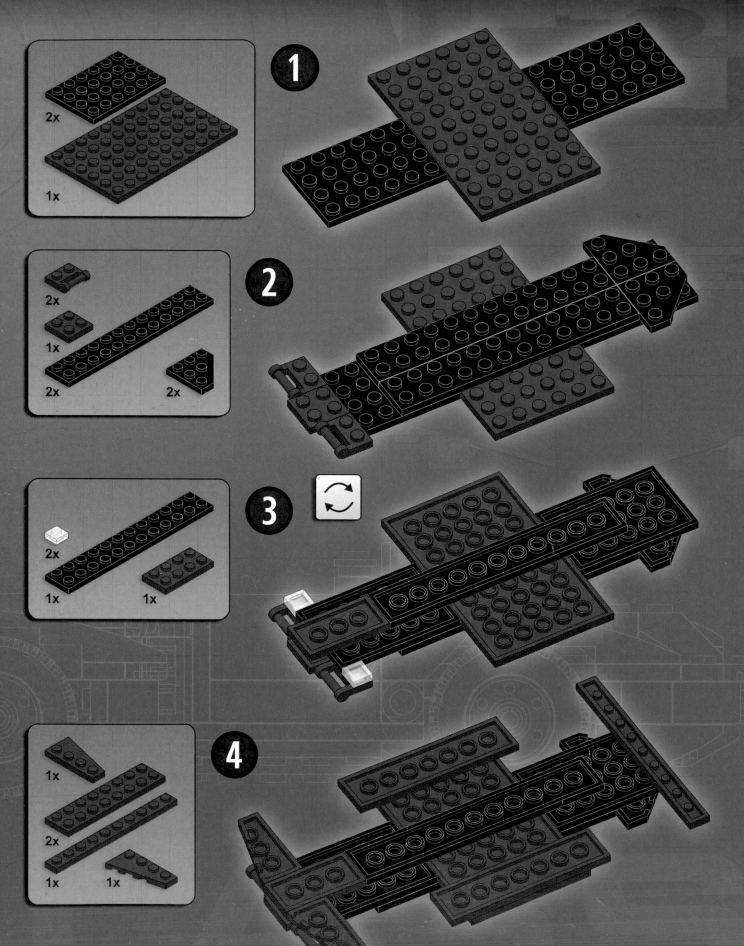

5

2x
1x 2x

6

2x
2x 6x
1x 2x

7

2x
2x

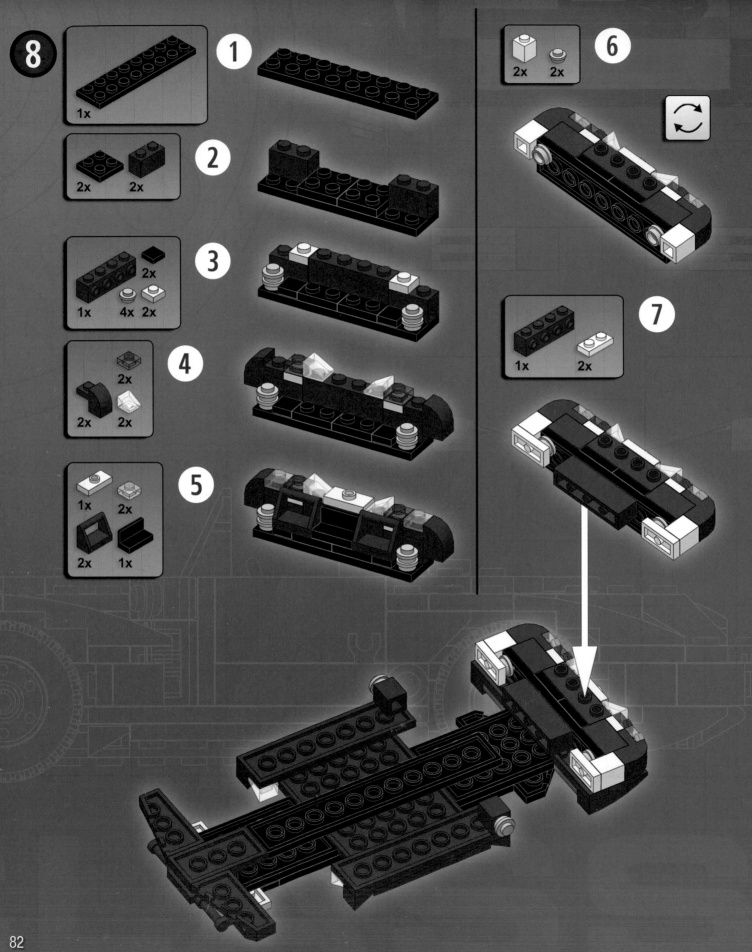

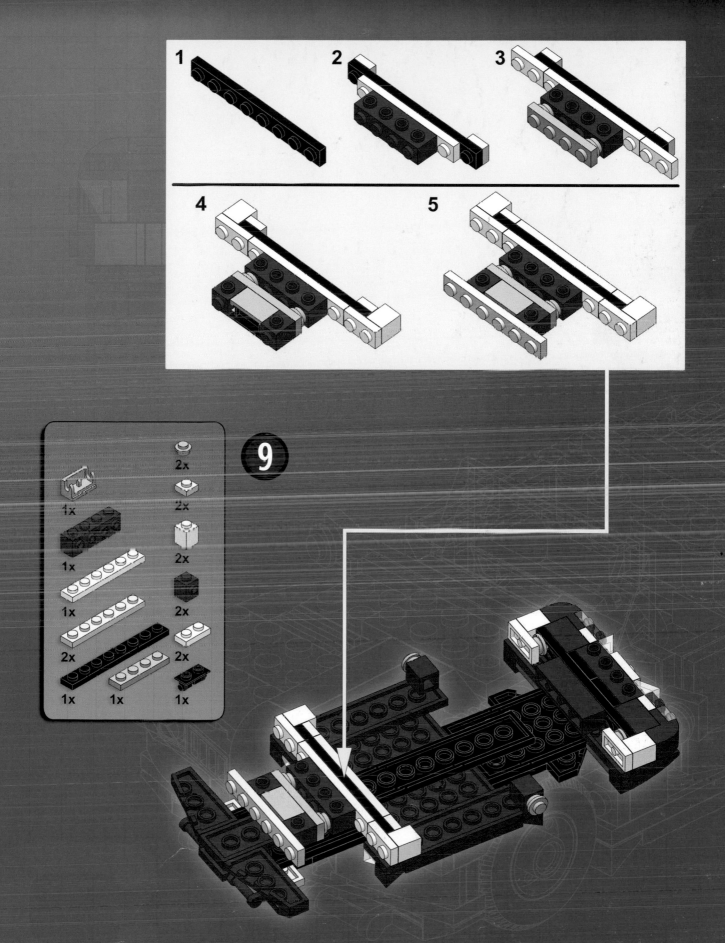

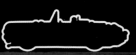

1   **2**   **3**

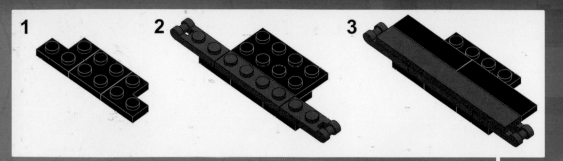

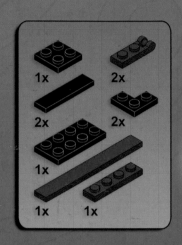

1x   2x
2x   2x
1x
1x   1x

10

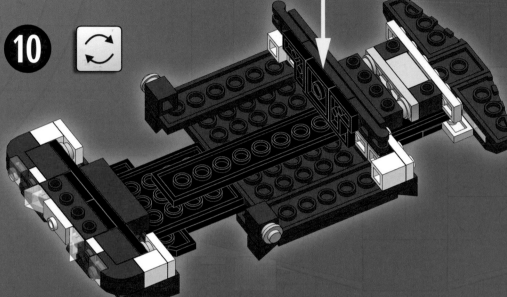

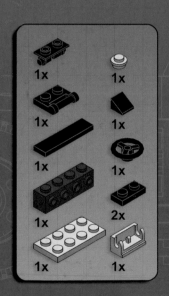

1x   1x
1x   1x
1x   1x
1x   2x
1x   1x

11

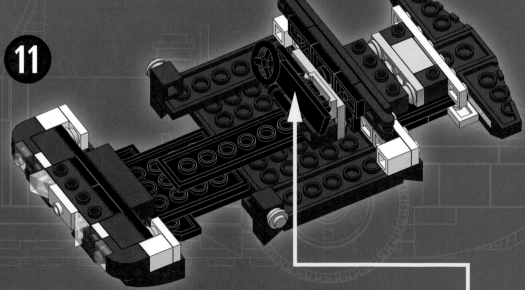

1   **2**   **3**   **4**   **5**

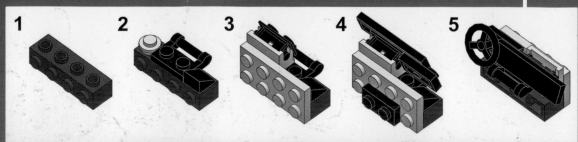

12

1

1x 2x

2

1x 2x

3

1x

1x

4

4x

2x 4x

2x 2x

1

2

3

1

2

3

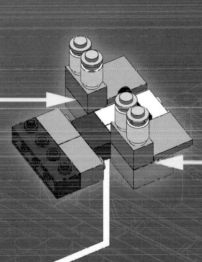

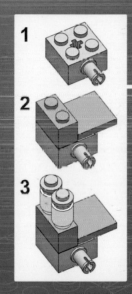

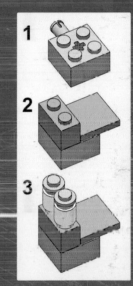

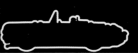

13

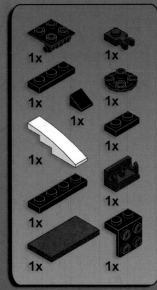

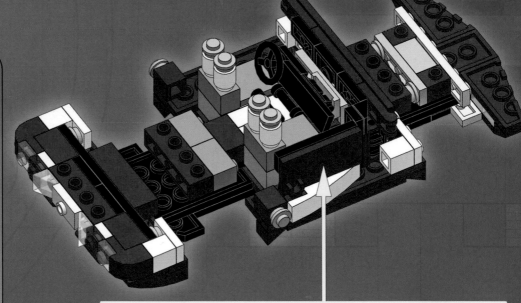

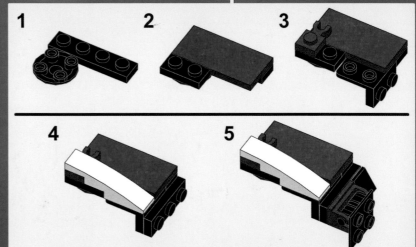

14

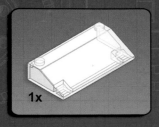

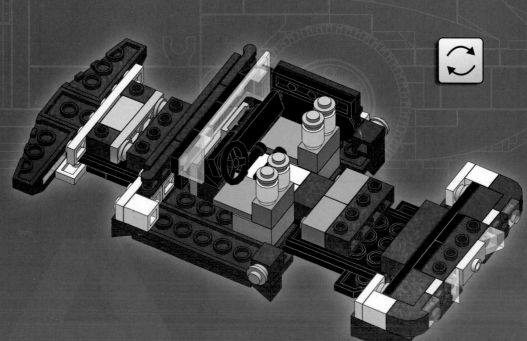

15

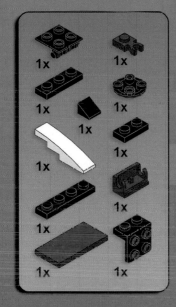

1x 1x
1x 1x
1x
1x 1x
1x
1x 1x

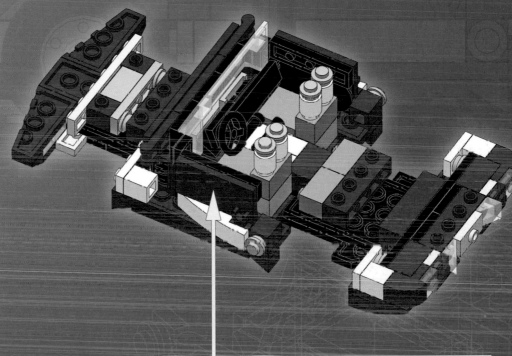

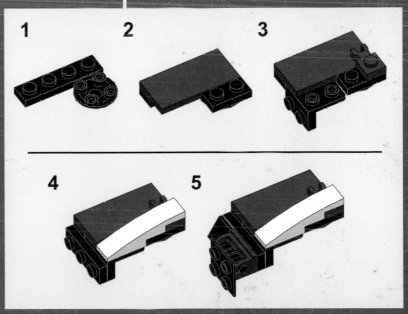

1 2 3

4 5

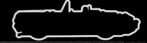

16

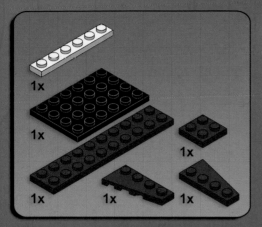

1x

1x

1x

1x 1x 1x

1

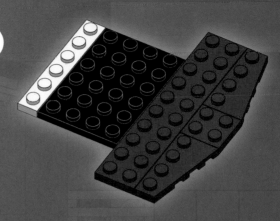

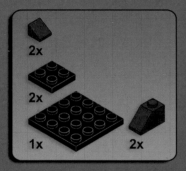

2x

2x

1x 2x

2

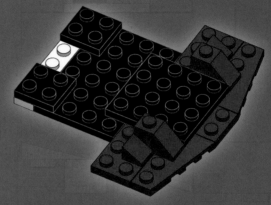

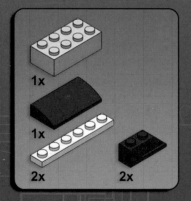

1x

1x

2x 2x

3

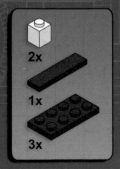

2x

1x

3x

4

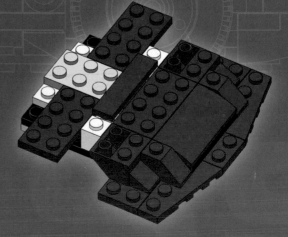

5

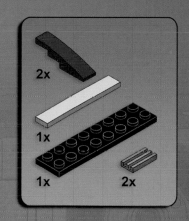

2x

1x

1x 2x

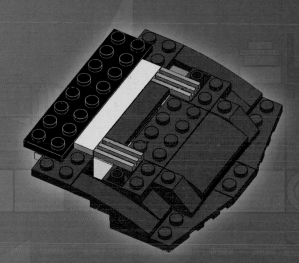

6

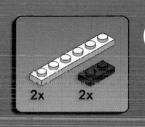

2x 2x

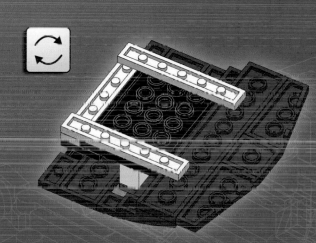

7

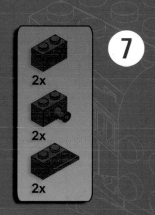

2x

2x

2x

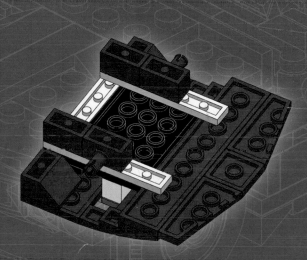

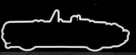

2x

8

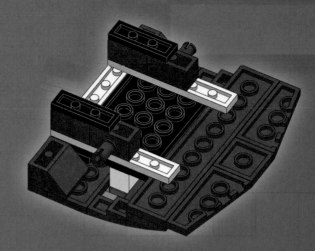

2x
1x 2x

9

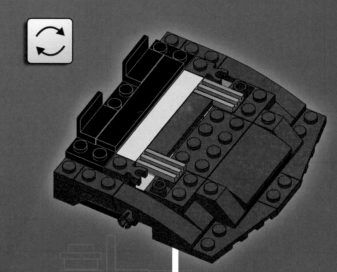

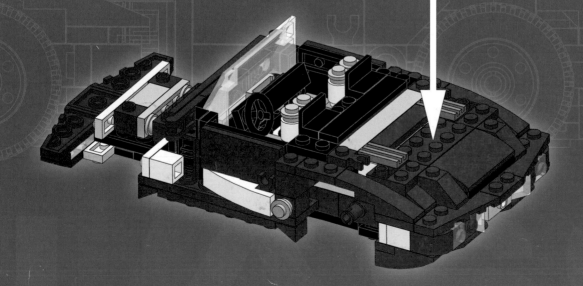

17

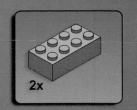

1

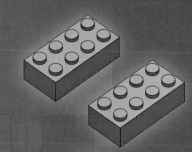

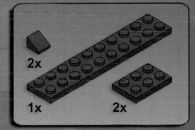

2

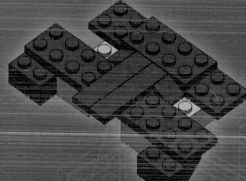

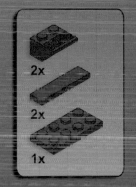

3

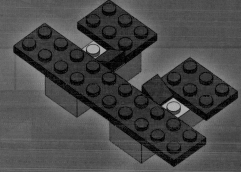

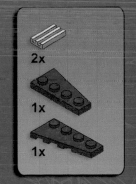

4

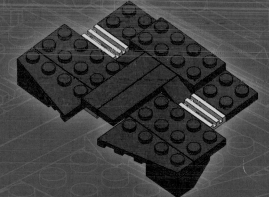

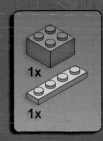

5

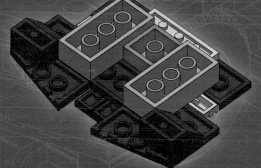

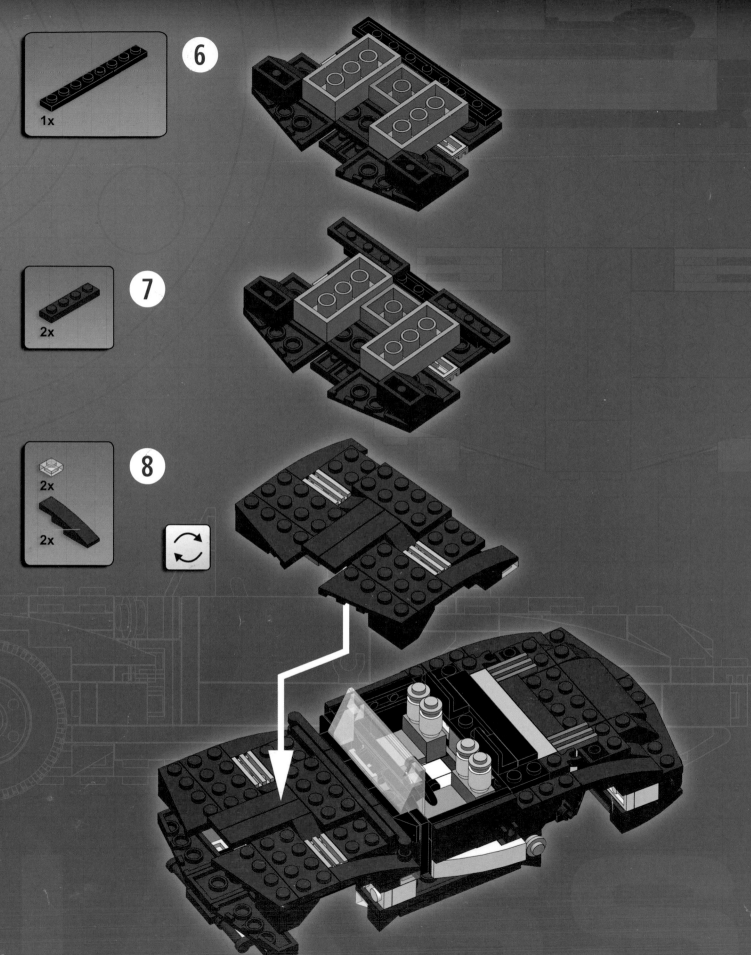

6 1x

7 2x

8 2x 2x

18

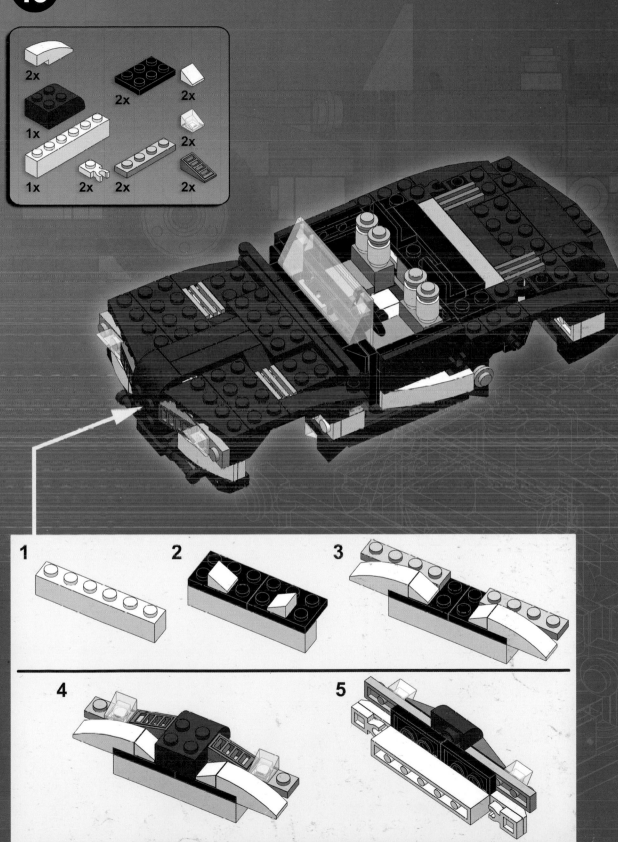

1

2

3

4

5

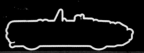

19

2x 2x 2x

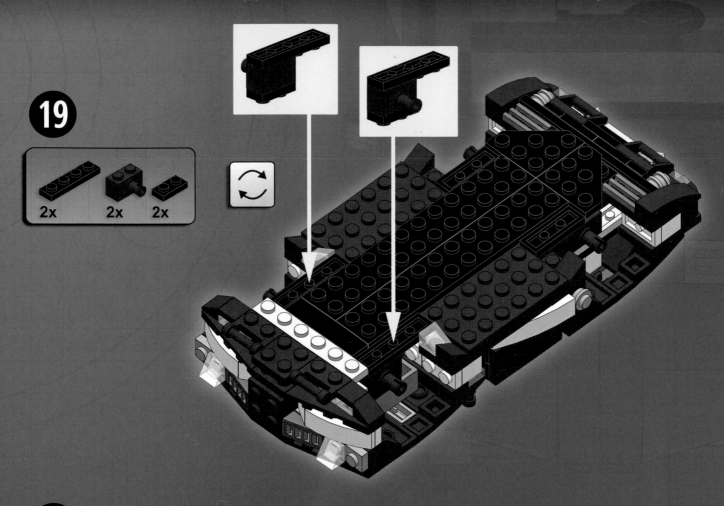

20

2x
2x
4x
4x

x2

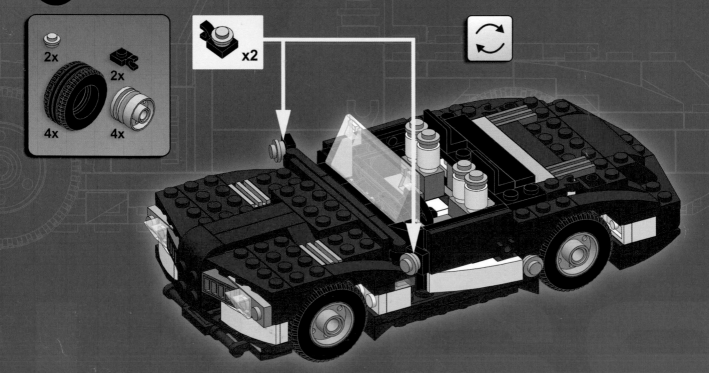

Complexity
Functions
Pieces

WHEEL LOADER

Design notes: heavy-duty construction, central cabin

Technical specifications:
Dimensions (l × w × h): 21 × 10 × 11 studs
Wheelbase: 9 studs
Axle width front/rear: 8/8 studs

Features: articulated steering, arm elevation, tipping bucket

1

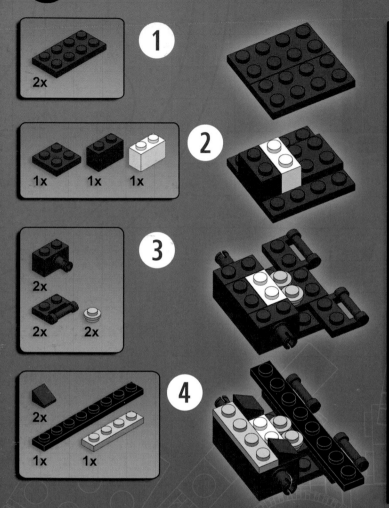

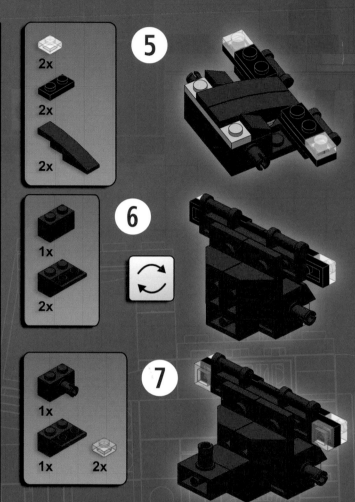

2

1
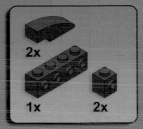
1x
1x

2
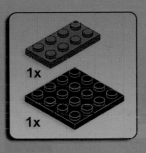
2x
1x   2x

3

1x
1x

4

1x
1x   2x

5
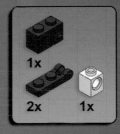
1x
2x   1x
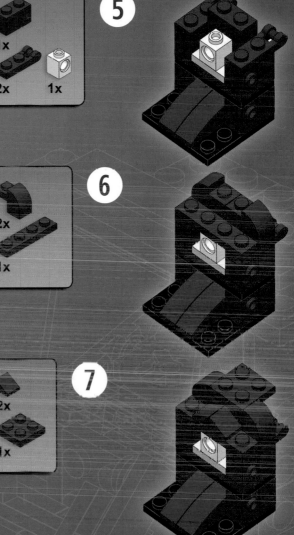

6
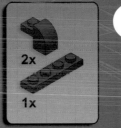
2x
1x

7
2x
1x

3

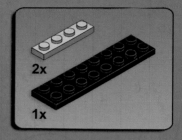
2x
1x

1

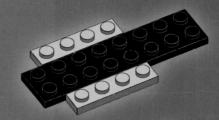

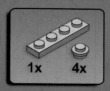
1x 4x

2

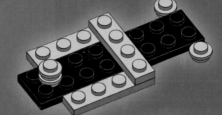

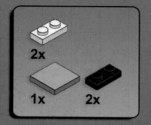
2x
1x 2x

3

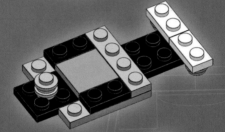

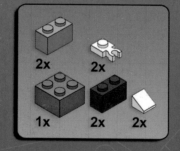
2x 2x
1x 2x 2x

4

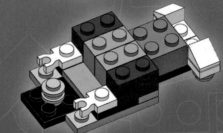

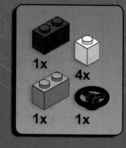
1x
4x
1x 1x

5

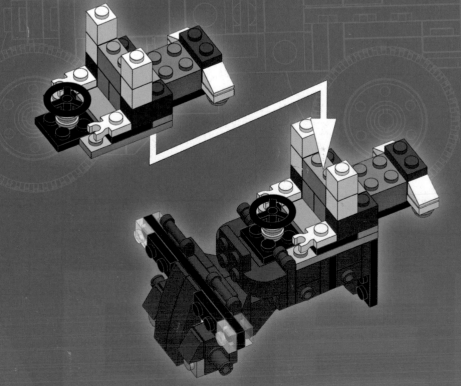

4

1x

1x

2x

1x

2x

1

2

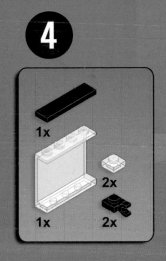

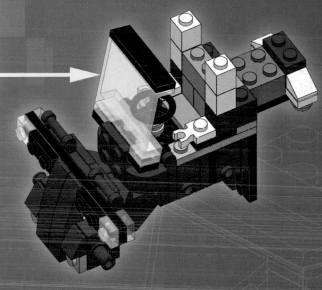

5

1x

1x

1x

1x

1x

1x

1x

1

2

3

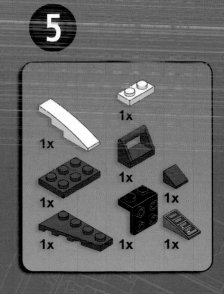
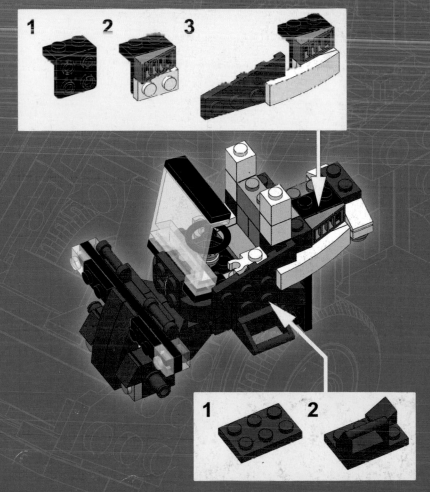

1

2

1   2   3

6

1x   1x
1x   1x
1x   1x   1x
1x   1x   1x

1   2

7

2x
2x   2x
3x
1x
2x
1x   4x

1   2

3   4

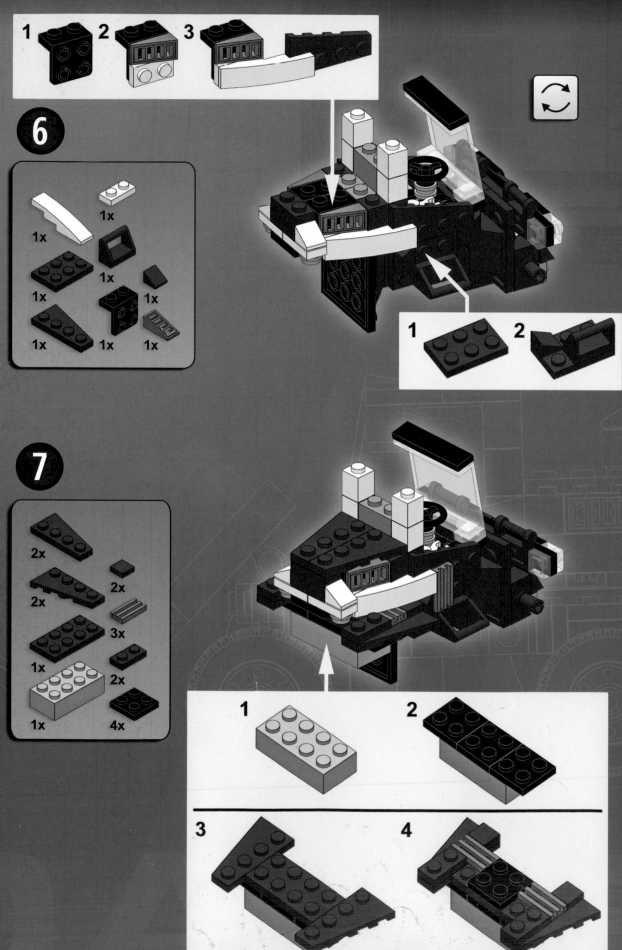

8

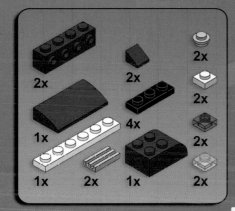

2x

2x

1x

1x 2x 1x

2x

2x

4x

2x

2x

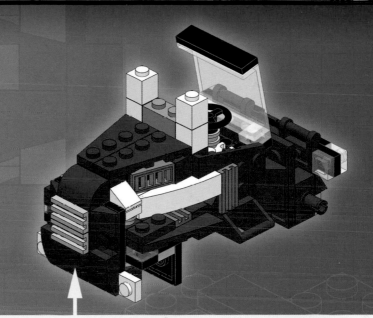

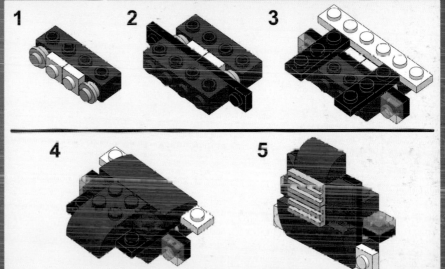

1 2 3

4 5

9

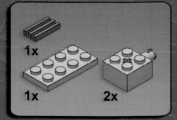

1x

1x 2x

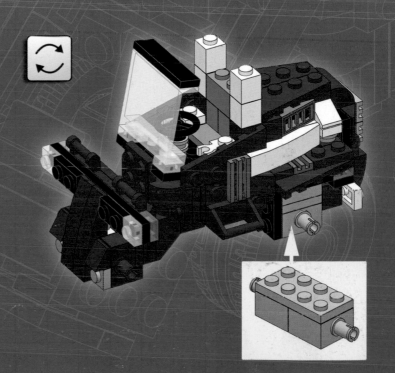

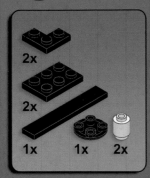

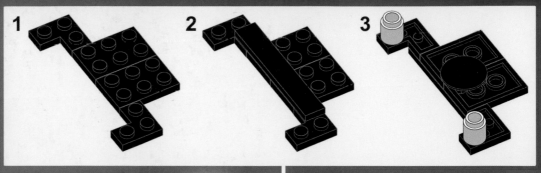

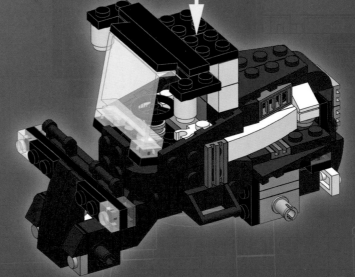

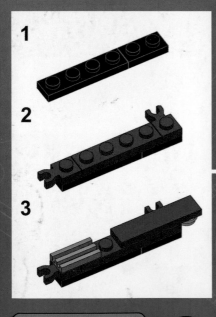

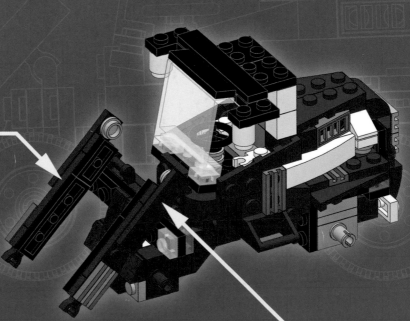

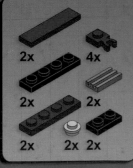

11

12

1

2x
1x

2

1x   2x   2x

3

2x   2x   2x

4

2x
1x   2x

5

3x   2x

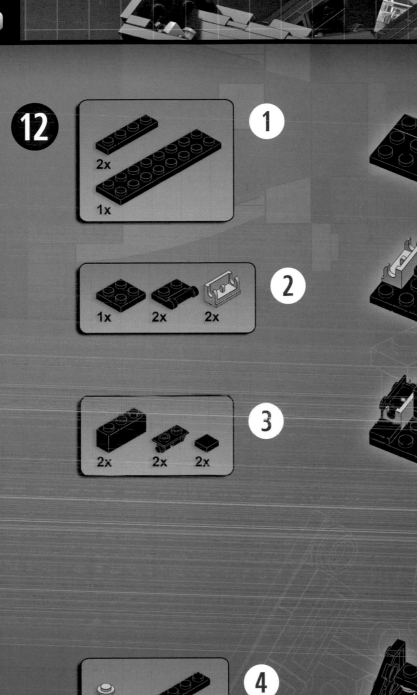
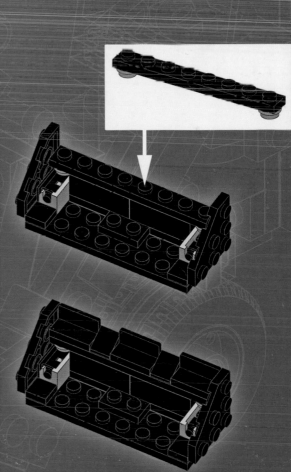

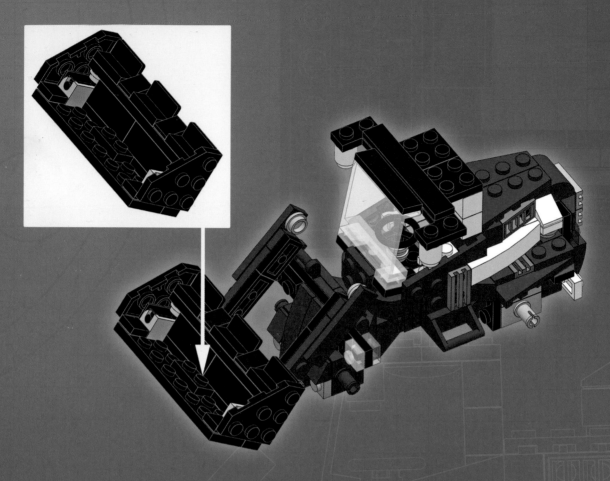

13

1x
1x
4x
4x

Complexity
Functions
Pieces

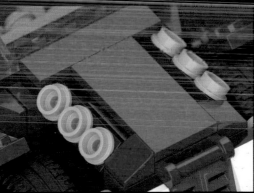

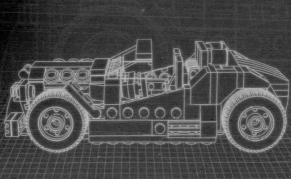

STREET ROD

Design notes: wide rear axle, lowrider, exposed V6 engine, detailed two-seat interior

Technical specifications:

Dimensions (l × w × h):	19 × 10 × 6 studs
Wheelbase:	12 studs
Axle width front/rear:	9/10 studs

1

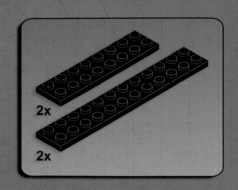

2x
2x

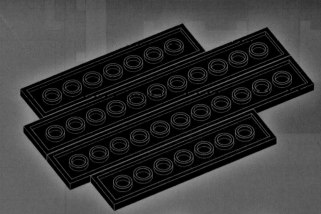

2

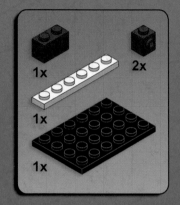

1x
2x
1x
1x

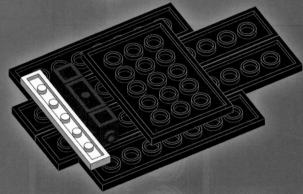

3

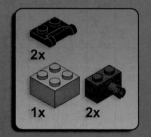

2x
1x   2x

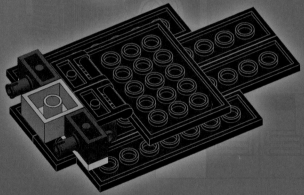

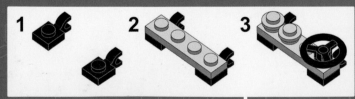

1   2   3

4

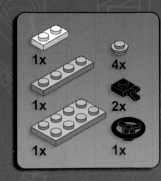

1x   4x
1x   2x
1x   1x

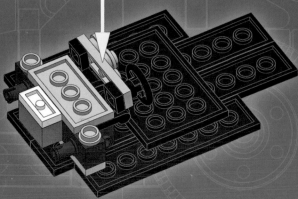

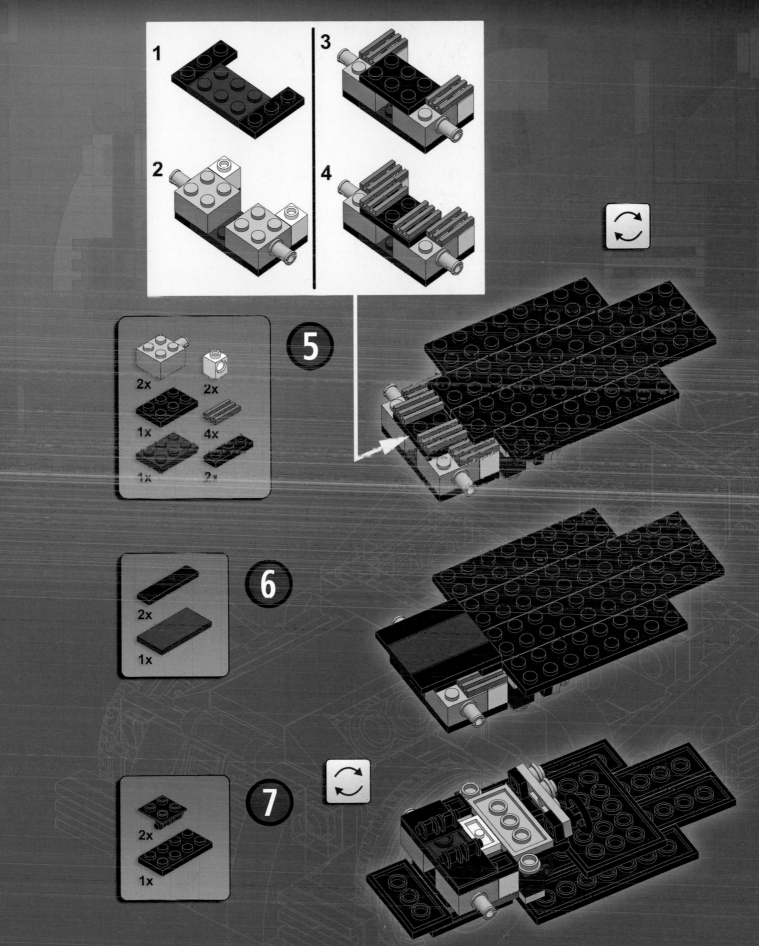

8

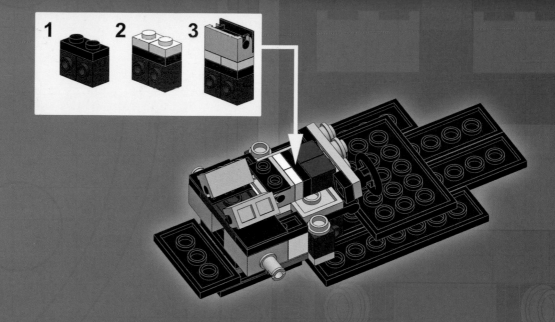

1 **2** **3**

9

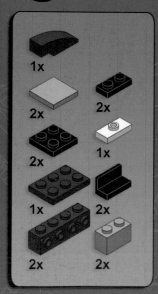

1 **2**

3 **4** **5**

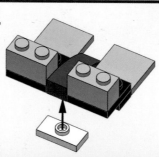
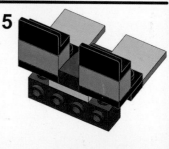

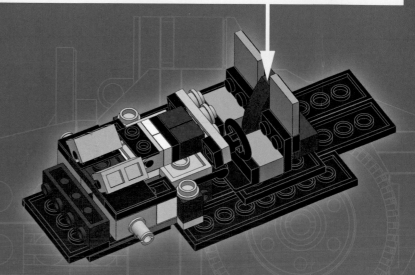

 3x

1

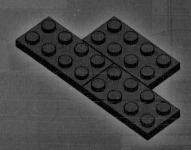

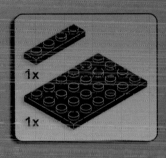 1x 1x

2

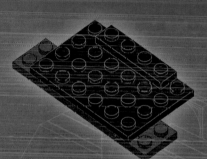

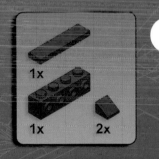 1x 1x 2x

3

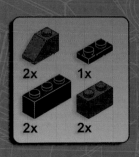 2x 1x 2x 2x

4

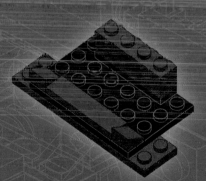

5

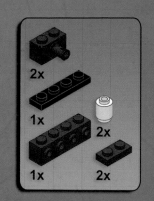

2x
1x
2x
1x
2x

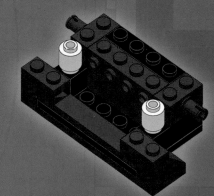

6

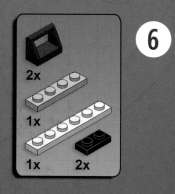

2x
1x
1x
2x

7

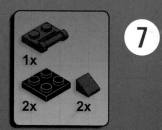

1x
2x
2x

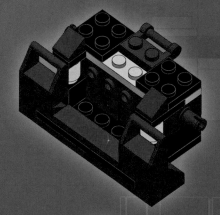

8

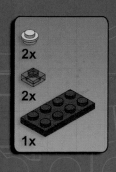

2x
2x
1x

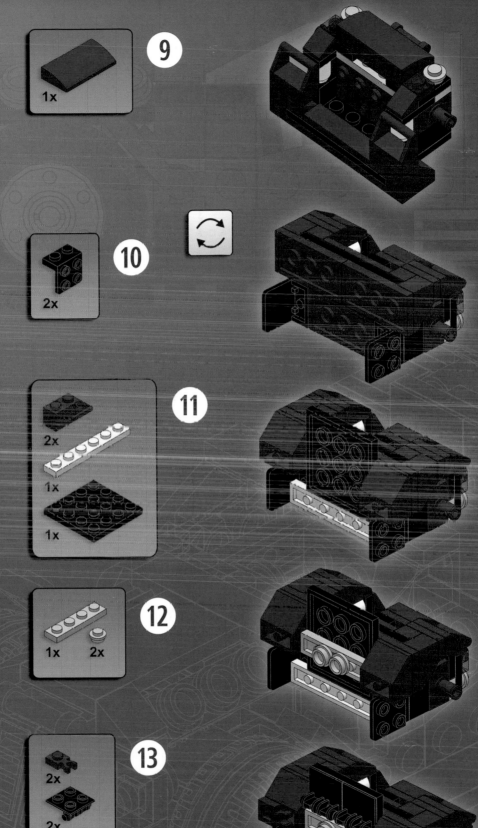

9
1x

10
2x

11
2x
1x
1x

12
1x 2x

13
2x
2x

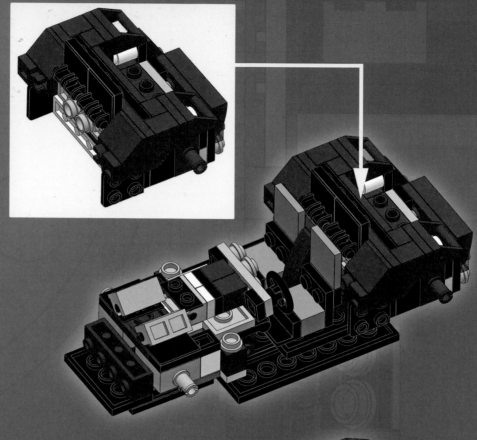

11

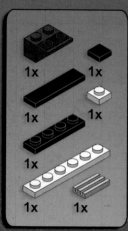

1x   1x

1x   1x

1x

1x   1x

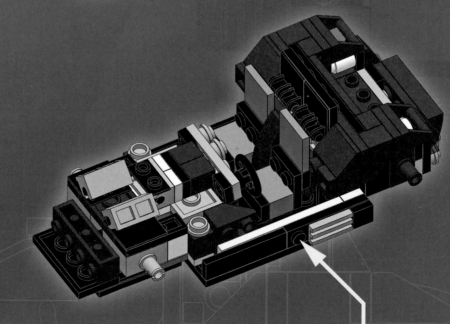

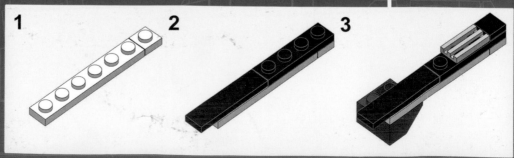

1   2   3

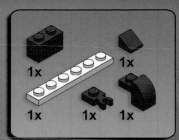

12

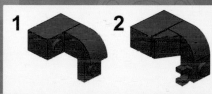
1x 1x 1x 1x 1x

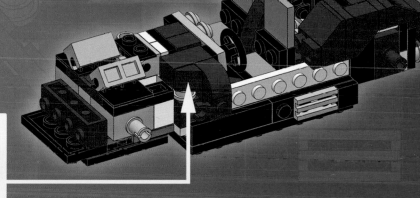

1 2

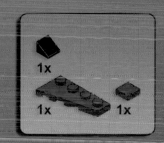
1x 1x 1x

13

14

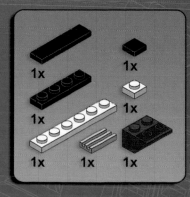
1x 1x
1x 1x
1x 1x 1x

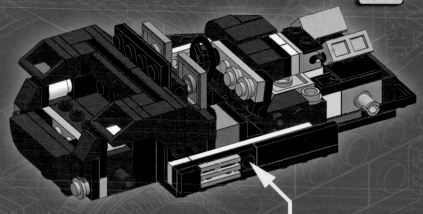

1 2 3

15

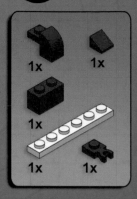

1x 1x

1x

1x 1x

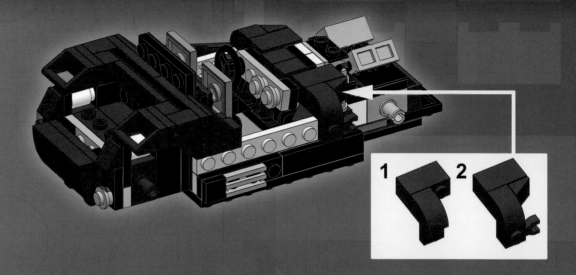

1 2

16

1x 1x

1x

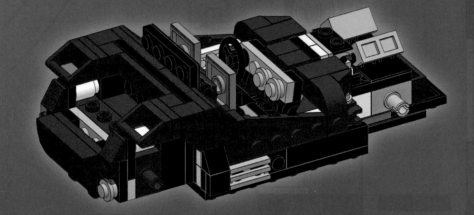

1 2

3 4

17

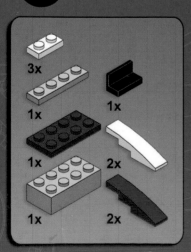

3x

1x 1x

1x 2x

1x 2x

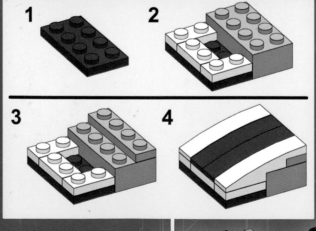

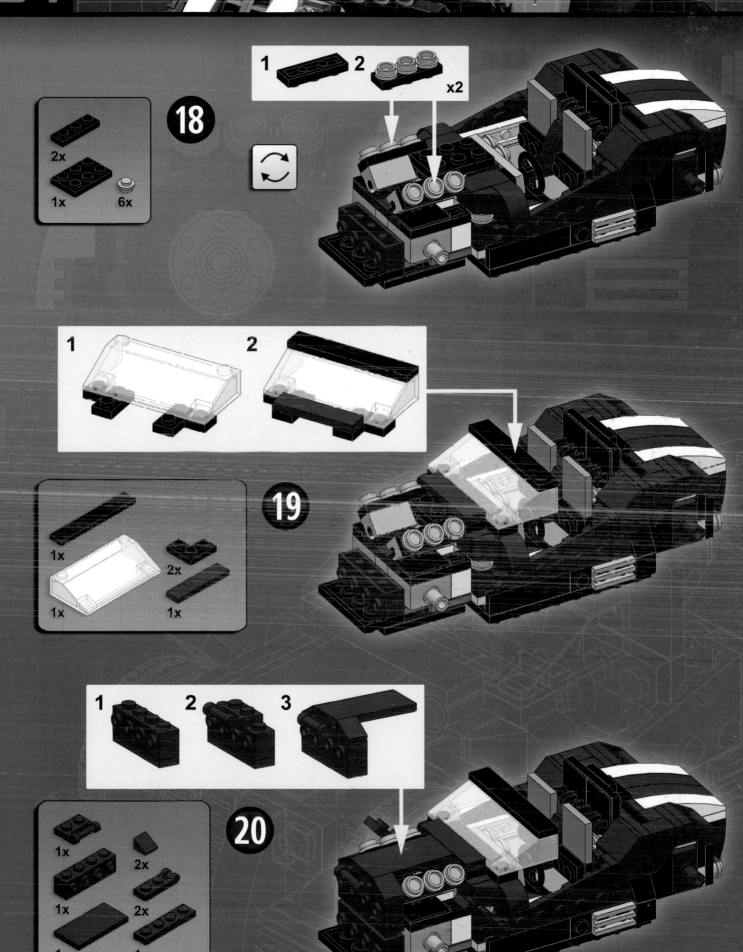

18

2x
1x   6x

1
2   x2

19

1x
1x   2x   1x

20

1   2   3

1x
1x   2x
1x   2x
1x   1x

21

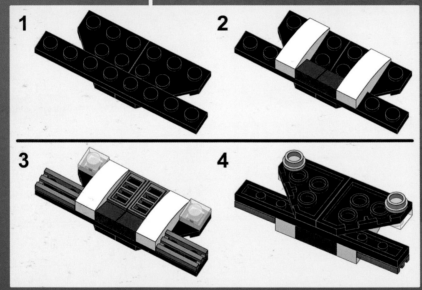

22

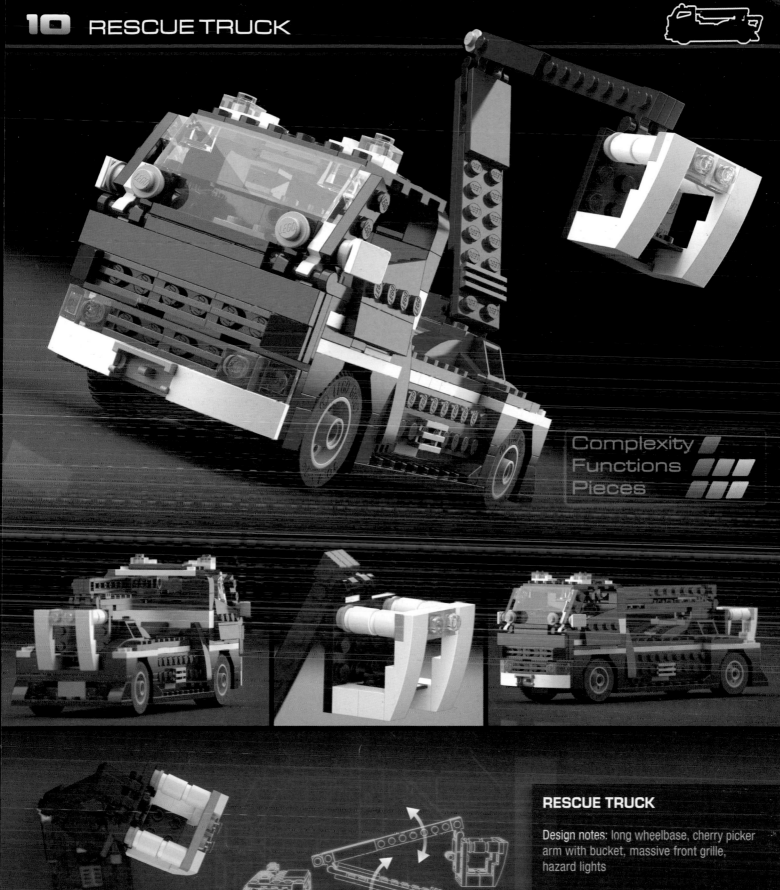

Complexity

Functions

Pieces

RESCUE TRUCK

Design notes: long wheelbase, cherry picker arm with bucket, massive front grille, hazard lights

Technical specifications:
Dimensions (l × w × h): 26 × 10 × 11 studs
Wheelbase: 16 studs
Axle width front/rear: 8/8 studs

Features: boom rotation, boom elevation

1

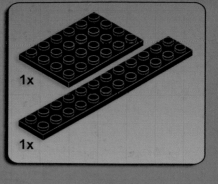

1x
1x

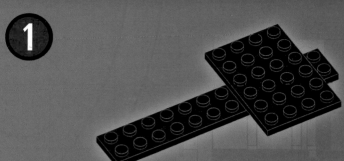

2

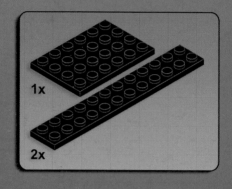

1x
2x

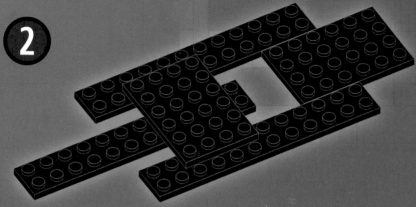

3

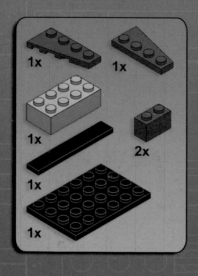

1x 1x
1x 2x
1x
1x

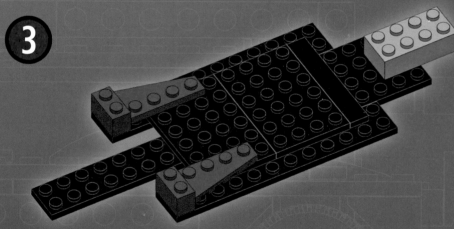

4

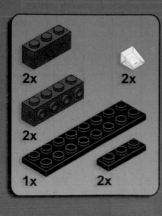

2x 2x
2x
1x 2x

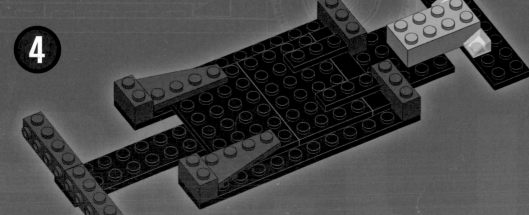

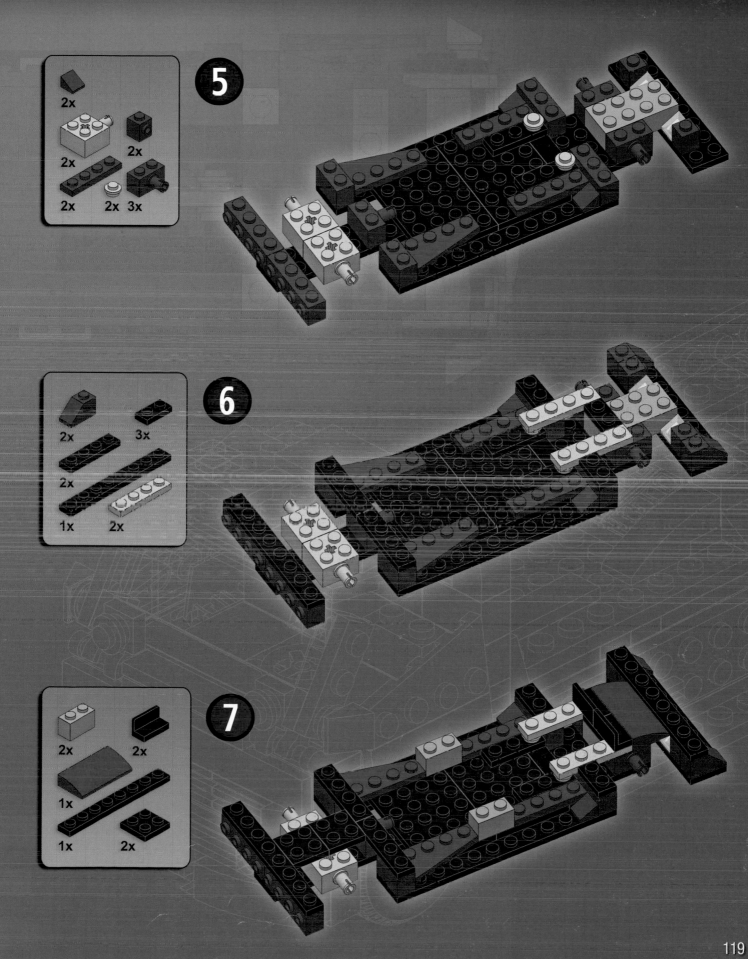

5

2x

2x 2x

2x 2x 3x

6

2x 3x

2x

1x 2x

7

2x 2x

1x

1x 2x

8

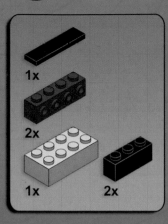

1x
2x
1x   2x

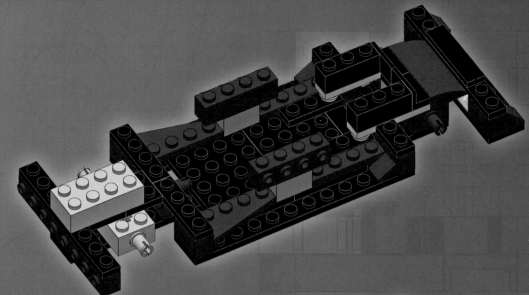

9

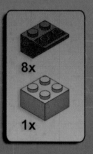

8x
1x

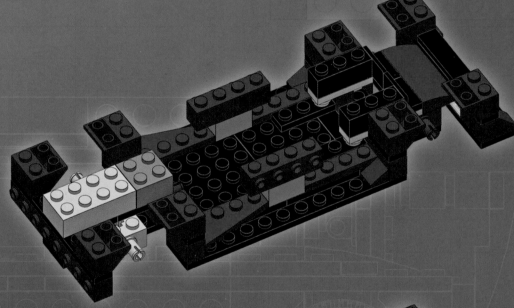

10

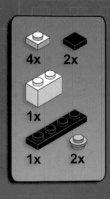

4x   2x
1x
1x   2x

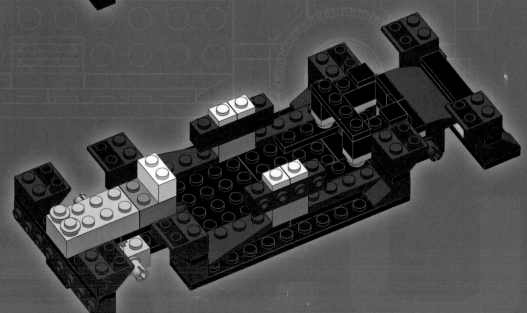

11

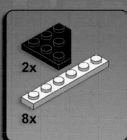

2x

8x

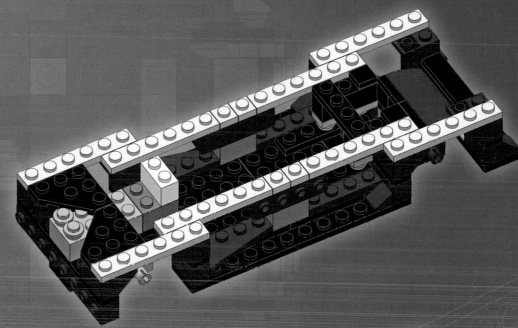

12

1x

2x

2x

2x

2x

1x

2x

2x

2x

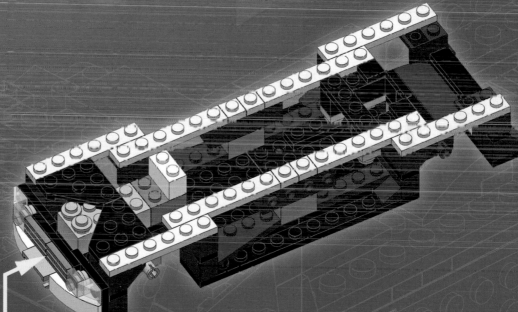

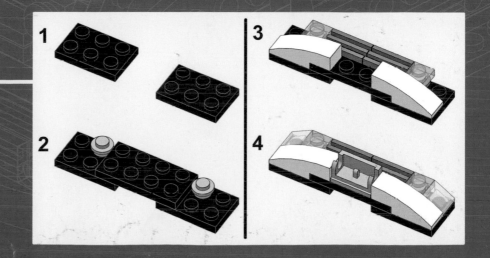

1

2

3

4

13

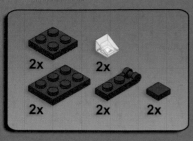

2x 2x
2x 2x 2x

14

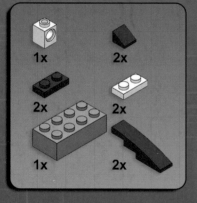

1x 2x
2x 2x
1x 2x

15

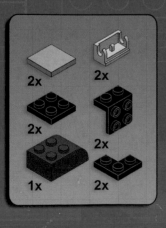

2x 2x
2x 2x
2x
1x 2x

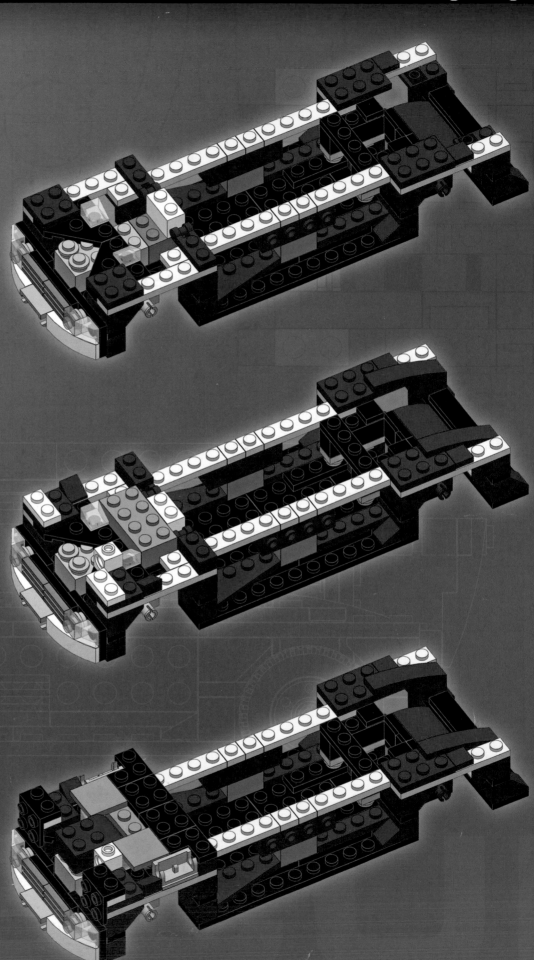

16

1x
1x
1x

2x

1x
1x

2x
2x

2x
2x
1x
2x

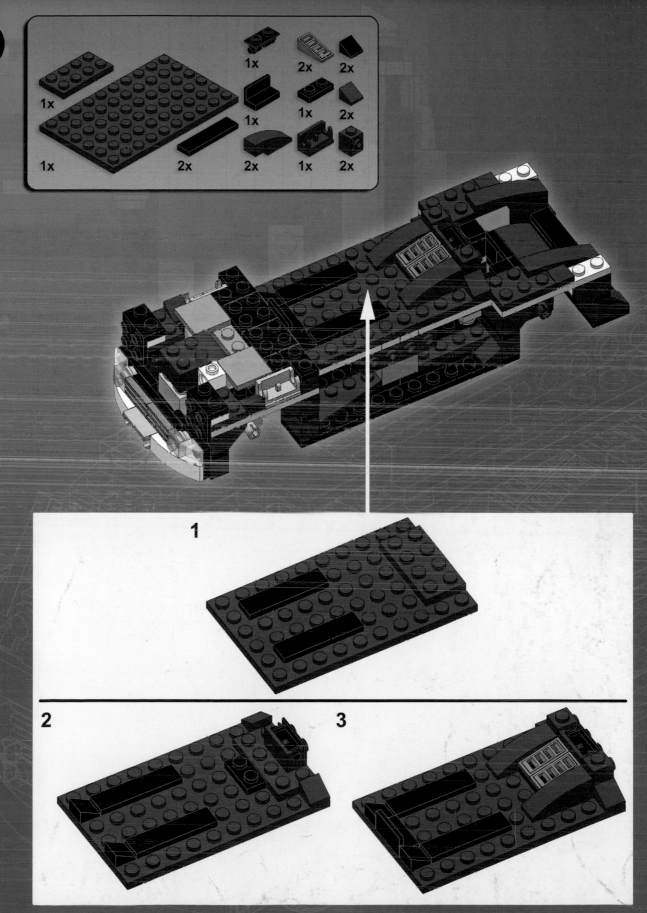

1

2

3

17

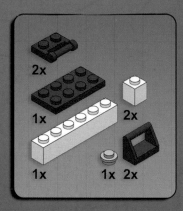

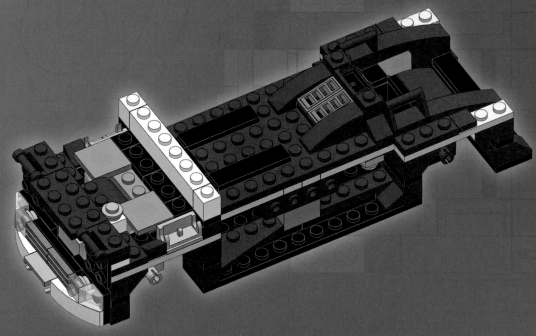

18

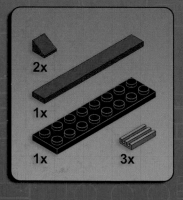

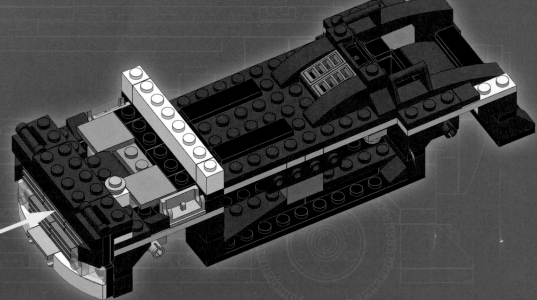

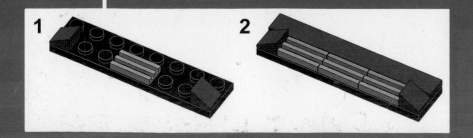

1

2

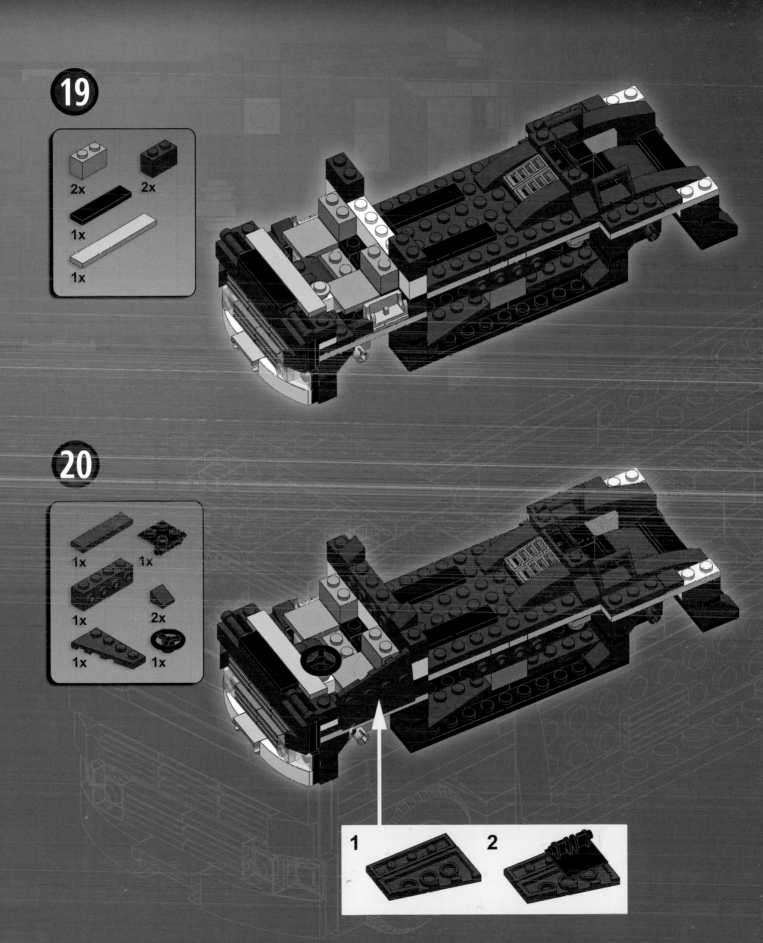

19

2x 2x 1x 1x

20

1x 1x 1x 2x 1x 1x

1 2

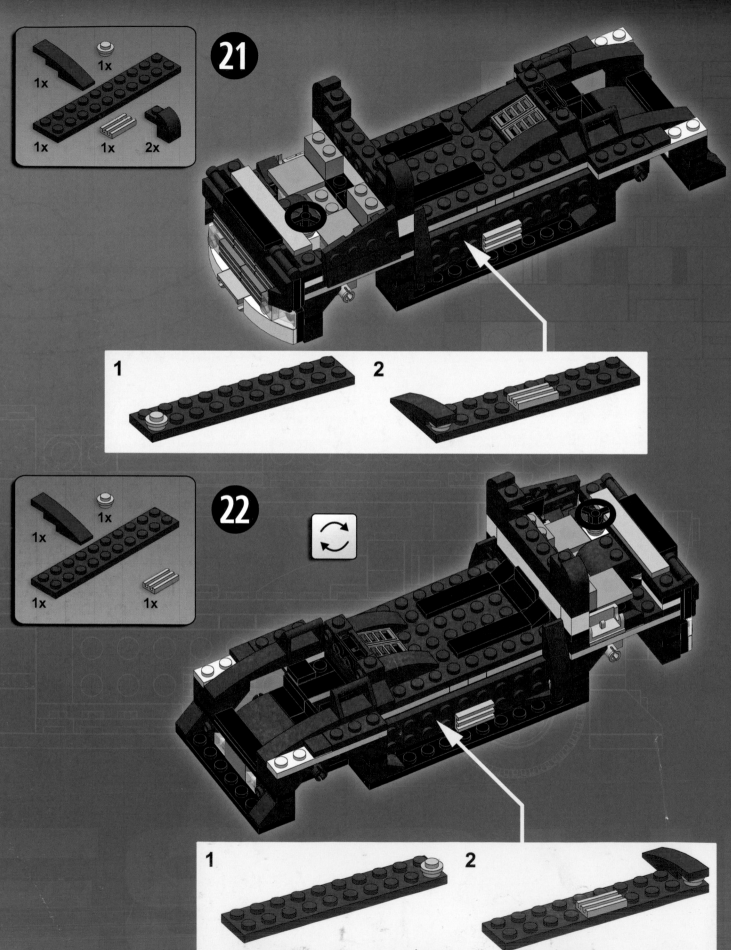

23

1x

1x

1x   2x

x2

1   2

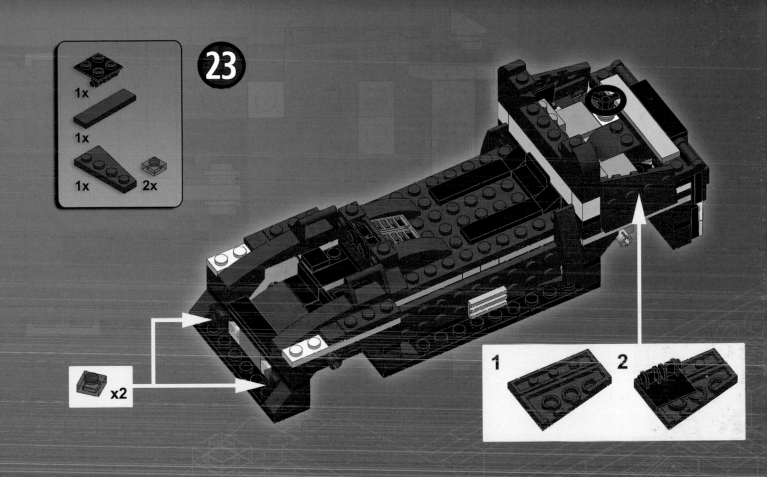

1   2   3   4

24

2x   1x

1x   1x

1x   2x

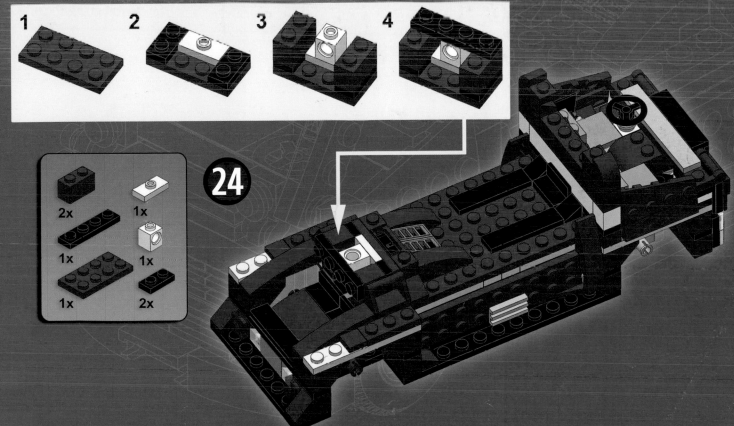

25

1x 1x

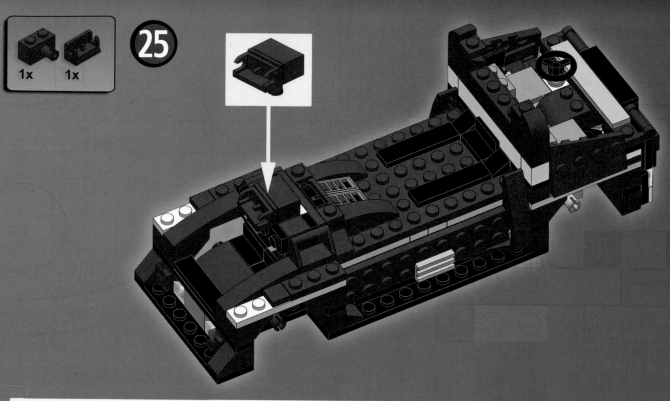

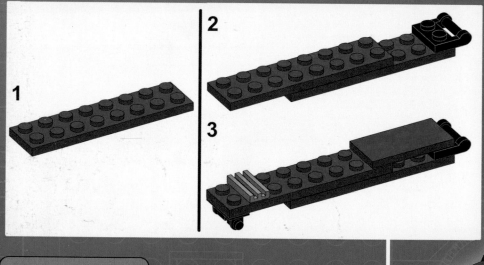

1

2

3

26

1x 1x

1x

2x 1x

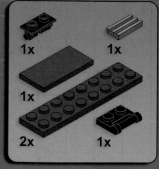

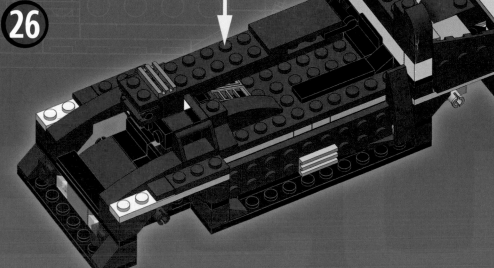

27

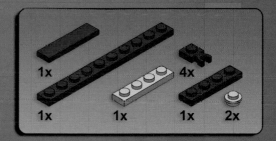

1x 4x

1x 1x 1x 2x

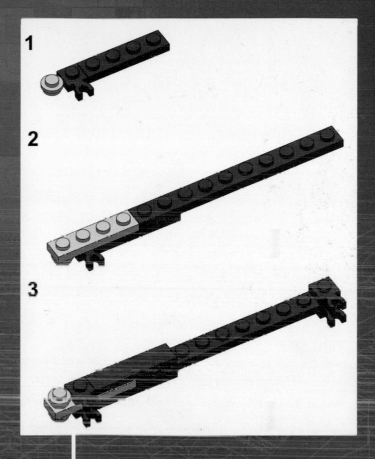

1

2

3

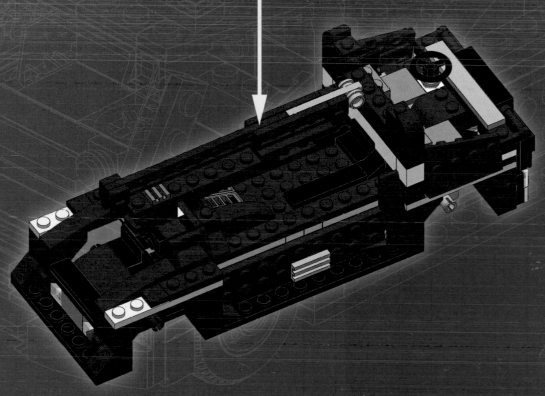

28

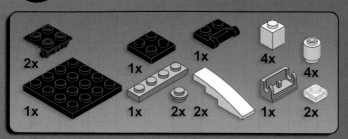

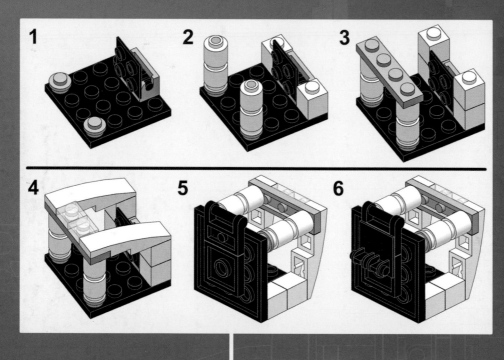

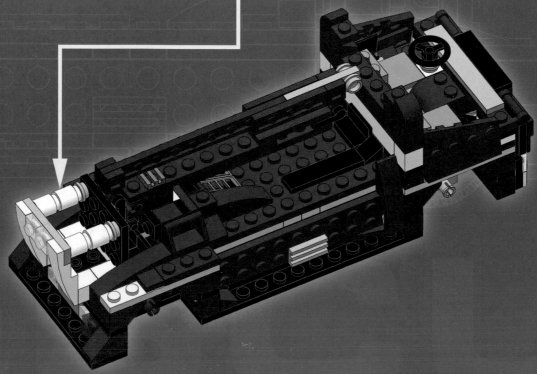

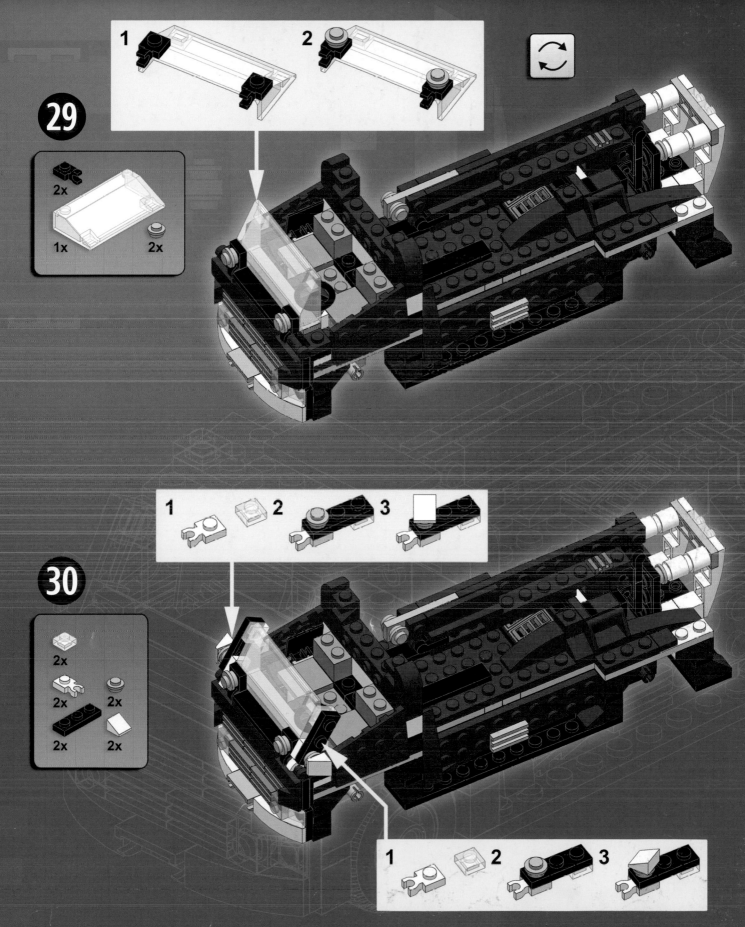

29

2x
1x   2x

30

2x
2x   2x
2x   2x

31

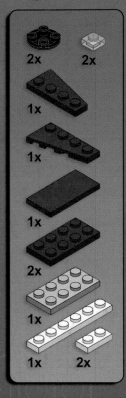

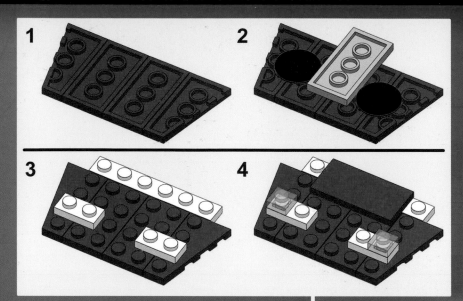

1

2

3

4

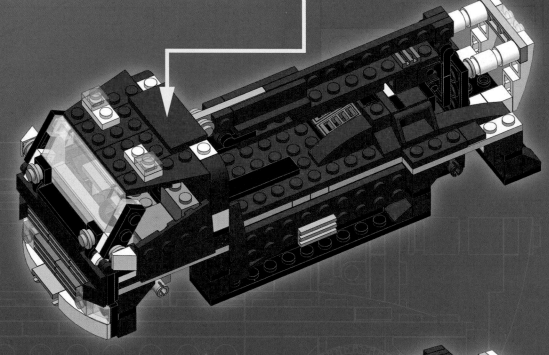

32

SAME BRICKS...
10 MORE STUNNING MODELS!
SEE YA!
DON'T MISS VOLUME 2!
VROOOOOM!!!

UPDATES

Visit *http://nostarch.com/builditvol1* for updates, errata, and other information.

More no-nonsense books from **no starch press**

THE LEGO® BUILD-IT BOOK, VOL. 2: MORE AMAZING VEHICLES

by NATHANAËL KUIPERS *and* MATTIA ZAMBONI
SEPTEMBER 2013, 152 PP., $19.95
ISBN 978-1-59327-513-6
full color

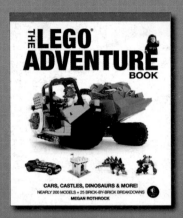

THE LEGO® ADVENTURE BOOK, VOL. 1: CARS, CASTLES, DINOSAURS & MORE!

by MEGAN ROTHROCK
NOVEMBER 2012, 200 PP., $24.95
ISBN 978-1-59327-442-9
hardcover, full color

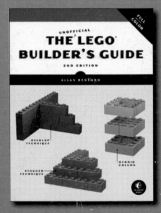

THE UNOFFICIAL LEGO® BUILDER'S GUIDE, 2ND EDITION

by ALLAN BEDFORD
NOVEMBER 2012, 240 PP., $24.95
ISBN 978-1-59327-441-2
full color

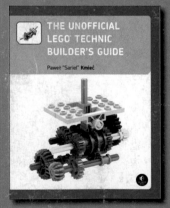

THE UNOFFICIAL LEGO® TECHNIC BUILDER'S GUIDE

by PAWEŁ "SARIEL" KMIEĆ
NOVEMBER 2012, 352 PP., $29.95
ISBN 978-1-59327-434-4
full color

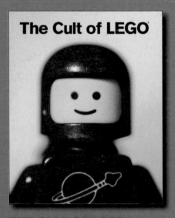

THE CULT OF LEGO®

by JOHN BAICHTAL *and* JOE MENO
NOVEMBER 2011, 304 PP., $39.95
ISBN 978-1-59327-391-0
hardcover, full color

THE LEGO® TECHNIC IDEA BOOK: SIMPLE MACHINES

by YOSHIHITO ISOGAWA
OCTOBER 2010, 168 PP., $19.95
ISBN 978-1-59327-277-7
full color

Visit *http://nostarch.com/catalog/lego* for a full list of titles.

phone: 800.420.7240 or 415.863.9900 | fax: 415.863.9950 | sales@nostarch.com | www.nostarch.com